FREE INDEED
EVEN FROM BEHIND BARS

C. ACUÑA

CLAY BRIDGES
PRESS

Free Indeed!
Even from behind Bars

Copyright © 2020 by C. Acuña

Published by Clay Bridges in Houston, TX
www.ClayBridgesPress.com

All rights reserved. No part of this publication may be reproduced, stored in a retrieval system, or transmitted in any form by any means, electronic, mechanical, photocopy, recording, or otherwise, without the prior permission of the publisher, except as provided for by USA copyright law.

Unless otherwise indicated, all Scripture quotations are taken from the New King James Version®. Copyright © 1982 by Thomas Nelson. Used by permission. All rights reserved.

Scripture quotations marked (ESV) are taken from the ESV® Bible (The Holy Bible, English Standard Version®), copyright © 2001 by Crossway, a publishing ministry of Good News Publishers. Used by permission. All rights reserved.

Scripture quotations marked (NASB) are taken from the New American Standard Bible® (NASB), Copyright © 1960, 1962, 1963, 1968, 1971, 1972, 1973, 1975, 1977, 1995 by The Lockman Foundation. Used by permission. www.Lockman.org.

Scripture quotations marked (NIV) are taken from the Holy Bible, New International Version®, NIV®. Copyright ©1973, 1978, 1984, 2011 by Biblica, Inc.™ Used by permission of Zondervan. All rights reserved worldwide. www.zondervan.com The "NIV" and "New International Version" are trademarks registered in the United States Patent and Trademark Office by Biblica, Inc.™

ISBN: 978-1-7352217-1-7
eISBN: 978-1-7352217-5-5

If anyone has questions about the author or the current status of his story, please contact Info@ClayBridgesPress.com. To protect the privacy of individuals, some names have been changed in the story. If you would like to inquire about or view the artwork from this book, please visit spiritbornepaintings.com.

Special Sales: Most Clay Bridges titles are available in special quantity discounts. Custom imprinting or excerpting can also be done to fit special needs. Contact Clay Bridges at Info@ClayBridgesPress.com.

This book is humbly dedicated to the following:

To Karen, my beloved wife, who through a labor of love, patience, and persistence kept me to the task at hand. She never lost sight of the vision God gave us, that I see myself as part of God's redemptive plan and beyond the circumstances I find myself in.

Malcolm, you are a dear brother in the Lord, and I thank you for your encouragement and steadfast prayer through my writing journey. You always pointed me back to the One who is able. I now know that baring my heart so others can have hope is in line with Who we are imitating.

Many thanks and blessings to the small yet powerful house church and their support for my family. You are all an incredible testimony of God's love. To Tim, our original pastor, whom God took home in the prime of his life, for simply speaking a word of faith into my life that, by the grace of God, has now come to pass.

To all the others who have poured their undying love and commitment into my life, there are simply no words. We'll discuss it in the hereafter.

Last but certainly not least, I am so grateful for the special people at Lucid Books who believed this book could become a reality before it was and, in so doing, believed in me. Your grace and faith have left an indelible mark on my life and on so many others.

TABLE OF CONTENTS

Chapter 1	Life in Costa Rica	1
Chapter 2	The Land of the Free	9
Chapter 3	Damaged Goods	15
Chapter 4	Too Many Mistakes	25
Chapter 5	The Vessel Begins to Crack (the Underbelly Is Ugly)	31
Chapter 6	The Past Meets the Present	39
Chapter 7	God Would Never Want Me	47
Chapter 8	The Worst Experience, the Best Result	53
Chapter 9	Angel to Me	61
Chapter 10	Deliverance Is a Journey	69
Chapter 11	Deliverance Is So Sweet	73
Chapter 12	What Now, God?	81

Chapter 1
LIFE IN COSTA RICA

My life in Costa Rica did not include the white, sandy beaches and turquoise-blue waters the typical American tourist talks about. It did not include ritzy resorts where people pay fixed prices to stay in gated and sometimes guarded communities. Nor did my life include guided horseback tours with gourmet lunches through the jungles to bird sanctuaries. I did not enjoy watered-down drinks with fancy umbrellas while floating in a resort pool rather than in the true outdoors filled with waterfalls, tropical fish, and fragrant flowers.

My earliest memories are dim and fuzzy. I do, however, remember the natural habitat of many insects, fish, and lizards since our bathroom was a hole in the ground down a dirt path, covered by banana leaves and grass, where insects and other creatures gathered to enjoy what we discarded there. Hot air—thick, humid, muggy, and clinging to everything—sums up an average day. Sometimes it rained for weeks or months on end. Tourists do not come during the rainy season. Depending on where we were living, there was little to do, and hours of boredom were hard to take. I could hear my father's bare feet shuffling around our one-room, raised dwelling on stilts. He busied himself by sharpening knives, whittling wood, and taking his time to roll and smoke a cigar. The oily, strong aroma of a tobacco leaf was unmistakable, and once lit, it made my stomach churn. Sometimes there was a break in the weather, if only for a day. Even in weather with temperatures of 95–100 degrees, my father drank hot coffee. He took boiling water from an old, blackened pot on the fire and poured it into a stainless-steel mug with recently crushed coffee beans at the bottom. Without a strainer, he sipped on this strong "cowboy" coffee constantly.

My memories until the age of six also include dusty roads, no shirt, ragged shorts, and bare feet. There was always a sensation of humidity in the air. I wore it like a cloak, anticipating an impending storm, even when the sun was beating down on my back.

My father, Juan, was a stocky man of mestizo descent—a combination of Spanish and native ancestry. I don't remember him having much hair, and it rapidly faded to baldness. The days were long when I ran after my father through tall fields of sugar cane. From the darkness of early morning to the darkness after sunset, he swung a machete back and forth as I ran around pretending to see friends among the cane, even though the stalks often cut my dark skin. I became weary, sometimes sleeping on my feet with nothing but a few sips of water and a crust of bread to eat.

Some days my father left me at home, and I would play outside with a couple of other children. Somebody's mother might give me a piece of fruit throughout the day. As the day went on, I hid in the corner of our hut in the dark, waiting for my father. Sometimes he returned dragging a large armadillo, a full jug of some strong-smelling liquid, a small package of chew, and some small bits of food for us to eat. It felt so good to have food in my belly. Sometimes we ate fish my father caught. But I also have very deep memories of him hurting me—I just don't know why. There are some painful feelings I have tried to forget over the years. My father never showed me love, and I remember the times he hit me for no apparent reason or knocked me to the ground without explanation. He was a drinker and spent a majority of the little money he made on liquor.

From my earliest memory, we ate one meal a day of rice and beans. Sometimes my father went into the rainforest and returned just as the sun was setting with a couple of fish. What a feast! Sometimes I was lucky enough to tag along with the understanding that I must stay back at a distance. I watched my father move rocks around to dam the brook and create a pool for the fish to check out. He sharpened a sapling and waited in the shadows of the trees until a fish came close enough for him to spear it.

I admire my father for his silent strength and rigorous work ethic. He worked a lot of land, clearing brush and loading a trailer with sugar cane. I can still hear that machete blade cutting through a stock of cane with a smooth whack. My brother Beto and I sometimes staked out the dirt path until we heard a tractor, and with folding knife in hand, Beto would hop onto the tail end of the trailer and yank one or two sugar cane poles (10 to 14 feet long) off the load. Then we would scurry into the jungle to enjoy the sugar cane water.

I remember walking down a long, dusty dirt road one day with my father when he abruptly stopped and leaned against a tree. Without hesitation or making a sound, he stuck the tip of his knife into the sole of his foot and twisted the blade. As I watched blood spurt out, he picked out a nail embedded in the sole of his foot. I guess it had been bothering him for some time, but I can't remember him grimacing in pain, let alone complaining.

My father moved us around a couple of times. I remember a place—a rectangular hut on elevated posts—that seemed remote to me. This hut had some sort of tin roof, and there were countless hours of what I now know as peace as I watched the rain come down and heard the pinging sound on the metal roof. We were surrounded by swamp and mangrove trees, and a small wooden ramp led us from the front door to a small clearing. One evening,

I witnessed a great battle there. As daylight was vanishing, the swamp was coming alive. I could never imagine what lurked below or around our hut and little clearing. My father heard something first and headed to the door with machete in hand. Through the fog and the smoky haze in our hut, I watched my father slip into the inky darkness, and I hesitantly made my way to the door. I could barely see the plank at the bottom of the stairs that ended at the clearing in front of our makeshift home. My father seemed to blend into the elements all around him, and I could see the brim of his hat slanted downward as if he were asleep. He was frozen in place, standing perfectly still.

Then I noticed what seemed to be a human-sized head on the ground, but it was actually an enormous frog. The size of a large boulder, this enormous frog was attempting to swallow a huge snake. The creature's body was thick, and it writhed left to right, only to stop as if rethinking its strategy. The snake was about 8 to 10 feet long. In the blink of an eye, my father took a step forward and brought his machete down, almost lightning fast, to cut the struggling snake in half. The frog happily waddled off with the snake's head, but strangely, the snake's other half slithered off in the other direction. My father headed back toward the house while I shuddered and ran to hide in the recesses of our dwelling.

My mother's name is Maria, and I hold on to one priceless memory of her. Beto, who is older by six or seven years, came one day to take me on a walk that would become a two-hour excursion through the jungle. We arrived at a clearing that offered us an awe-inspiring view of a raging river (in my young eyes). The recent rains had stained the boulders dark brown, and there was a wooden deck on which a woman stood washing clothes. I knew at once that this was not some random villager washing clothes in the river—she was my mother. After years of waiting and wondering, this quiet, simple woman Beto had brought me to see was my mother. I almost felt her hot tears long before I reached her. She embraced me and held me close, smelling clean, warm, and safe. This is where I came from. She had long, flowing, brown hair that enveloped me in a soft, sweet place I longed to stay. At one point, Beto ran down to the dock, and I followed, as always. I peered into the water and then slipped in for what seemed like a long time, but it was probably only a few seconds. Looking up, I saw Beto's large hand coming down to grab me. Because of this experience, I would have an aversion to dark, cold water for years to come. That was the first and last time I remember seeing my mother.

I often watched my father milk the cows in the shade of some trees by a pasture. He beckoned me over and sprayed milk into my mouth. I remember walking back to our dwelling with a pail full of milk. My father skimmed off the fat on top, and then we took gulps of fresh, warm milk. This is a soothing memory, much like the memory of my birth mother, Maria.

One day, I was sitting in the road playing by myself. I must have been six. This long dirt road was the only way in and out of the land my father worked. A small, white pickup truck rolled by, and its driver stopped just long enough to ask, "¿Dónde está tu padre?" (Where is your father?) I pointed farther up the road where he was working in a field of sugar cane. After a while, the truck left where my father was. The next time it came, the men picked me up, put me into the truck, and kept me occupied with a folder and a paper clip while we drove out to the fields. I can still see it clearly in my mind today. The sun was blazing hot, scorching my father's weathered back. All I could hear were the insects buzzing and the *thwack, thwack, thwack* of his machete swinging back and forth in the sugar cane. One of the men got out to talk to my father, but it was only a few minutes and then we were leaving.

As we drove away slowly, I looked out the rear window. My papa had stopped working and seemed to be standing perfectly still like a rock statue. The sun was on his back as I had seen so many times before, and I could barely see his face. I'd like to say I saw a single tear streaming down his face as we tried to lock eyes. The window of time was closing. We were getting farther and farther apart. In that moment, I realized we would never see each other again.

The men took me to an orphanage in the hills of San Jose. The first person I met there was Padre Wayne, the man who ran the place. He told me he was everyone's father—papa to all. This notion confused me. How could that be possible? I wandered around quietly and kept to myself. I had never worn shoes or seen a book, let alone played with or seen this many children. One day I was called to Papa Wayne's office where he introduced me to a little girl named Rebecca Rose and a little boy named Antonio Carlos. He told me they were my brother and sister. They were younger than I and so adorable that I happily embraced this idea of instant family. We spent about a year at the orphanage with amazing people who fed and provided for us. We had wonderful experiences, like trekking through the rain forest and going through what remained after earthquakes. One time when I was in a room full of bunk beds and about 16 to 18 boys around my age, there was an earthquake I will never forget. I woke up to a grinding sound and a crack forming in the ceiling above my head. The ground was shaking, and it was hard to stand. Everyone was yelling for us to get outside. I glanced out the window and saw trees and bushes cracking and moving everywhere. Was it a good idea to go outside? During a later earthquake, a large crack swallowed up an entire swing set.

One night, I awoke to feel an unexplainable sensation in the air. It was dark, humid, and silent. All I could hear was the breathing in the room—no insects or birds, just silence. I was lying on my right side facing a shaft of light that came into the room from the bathroom across the hall when I sensed something behind me and felt the air become very cool. I turned to look, and there about a foot from my face was a black human hand. It was about three feet in the air and perfectly still. I was terrified—I couldn't scream but was frozen in fear. After staring in terror for a moment at the hand, I pulled my sheets over my head. I thought maybe my bunkie was messing with me, but when I called out, there was no response. He was fast asleep. My heart thumping in my little chest, I finally began calling out to anyone for help. When no one responded, I decided to peek out. The black hand had completely vanished. Years later, I learned that this symbol, the Black Hand, or Mano Negra, is a multipurpose calling card of devil worship, voodoo, and black magic, and a sign used by some drug cartels, assassins, and hit men before a murder. It was never viewed as a good thing if you encountered a black hand in any way, shape, or form. Strangely, about 13 years later, my own left hand would be slashed in a struggle over a knife in a black car. I would then be charged with murder.

There is one more memory I believe left a mark on me for many years to come. Occasionally, a young teenage girl led me into the nursery and masturbated in front of me. She also laid me down to perform oral sex on her. Although I was only seven and had no idea what was going on, I did know that this was something secretive and prohibited.

Eventually, this orphanage closed after the number of children dropped from 50 or 60 to about five or six. Papa Wayne adopted some of the orphans, including the teenage girl, and the rest of us went to another orphanage in the capital city of San Jose. There were iron bars and grills on the doors and windows, and the front gate was always locked. One day, an American family showed up, and my sister, brother, and I were called in to meet them. We spoke for about 20 minutes. The lady spoke better Spanish than the man. A couple days later, they returned and took us to McDonald's for lunch. I had become accustomed to eating "real" food at Papa Wayne's, but this was different. I think they saw it as a treat, but I had never seen such a place. They visited us one more time at the orphanage, and then one day they drove us to a villa on a hillside of San Jose.

It was a memory that made a significant impression on me—being in a large, open room in the villa that Ann and John, my soon-to-be adoptive parents, had rented. It was like nothing I had ever seen, with one wall of large cubes of green, tinted glass and beautiful french doors. There was a cook who was always busy preparing delicious food for us to eat. One evening after supper, I came out of the hallway and into the common room to see my little brother (age four) half sitting, half leaning on Ann's lap. Her shirt was pulled up over her shoulder and Antonio's mouth was fixed on her breast. I stopped and stood still, transfixed by what I was seeing. I was confused and curious. I did not have a sense of this being acceptable or familiar. I could not recall seeing let alone touching a breast with my mouth. My neck burned and my heart pounded as my mind raced back to that riverbank. Did I nurse on my mother's breasts?

My sister, Rebecca, wandered in, and I tagged along to the couch. Rebecca (age six) was offered a turn, but I was not. Was I too old, too awkward? Ann shook her head slightly at me and covered up, and then we sat on the couch and played games.

Ann was a stay-at-home mom, and John worked in computer technology. We were living a life of luxury with a cook, a gardener, and a pool all to ourselves, and we also met our soon-to-be great-grandma. John had to return to America early for work, but the rest of us spent two to three weeks at the villa. One day we visited a couple of restaurants and went down to the market with Ann, and I could not believe how much food there was, all in one place. On another occasion we took a caravan tour of the Irazú Volcano, which was a short distance outside the capital. It was an amazing sight!

Chapter 2
THE LAND OF THE FREE

My adoptive parents decided to adopt since they were unable to conceive children. In October 1991, they adopted me (age seven), my sister (age six), and my brother (age four). It must have been overwhelming for them to have three young children all at once.

My first couple years in America were not so bad. I did not know or understand a word of English for the first year or so. We did not go to English classes or meet other children. The change was abrupt. America was a new country with a new language, and we were in a new household with parents who had little understanding of the ways of children. This was not my choice.

I became angry at my new parents for uprooting me and transplanting me into a completely foreign culture with little emotional support. It must have come as a surprise when they learned I had emotional wounds caused by abuse in the past. I believed this move was a temporary situation, a vacation in America, but I was sadly mistaken. I did not grasp the concept of authority, and it was a struggle for me to respect and obey these strangers who had become my parents. This led to seeds of bitterness and discontentment sown early in my life.

In Costa Rica, I had run around barefoot with no shirt. Overnight, I was wearing underwear, a shirt, well-starched and pressed pants, socks, and shoes. I felt like a donkey packed with a saddle and laden down with goods for the market. We also attended church, a medium-sized congregational church, every Sunday. We were often dressed almost the same as neatly wrapped packages. Ann sewed our clothes and homeschooled us. We never fit in.

I don't remember if the gospel was preached. It may have been, and I would never want to detract from anyone serving the Lord at that church, but my concern was the discomfort of my toes squished into my shoes and the tie tied tightly around my neck. I was not permitted to move or leave Ann's line of sight. God forbid that any of us should act like a child and bring embarrassment to Ann. We were never permitted to play with other children, loosen our ties, or go barefoot. I began to learn that our lives were to be subject to her ultimate control.

As we all conformed to church life and homeschooling, we also conformed to other household practices. After we had been in America for a year or two, I remember standing awkwardly in the shower with one or both of my parents, the smell of body wash wafting through the air. Sometimes it would be one of us kids, sometimes two. I was eight or nine by then. The bathroom on the second floor off their bedroom was strictly off-limits. While we bathed, I remember looking at my parents' faces to read their emotions, but they were always passive, nondescript. Then I would look down at their private areas. My parents' nakedness being uncovered to me brought feelings of shame and embarrassment, and I sometimes cringed when they hugged me as my mind swirled at the thought of us naked together in the shower. As a child in Costa Rica, I yearned to be held to a mother's chest to hear her heartbeat and nestle my face in her breasts, even if it was not the mother who birthed me. I never had that nurturing or attachment with Ann. Confusion flooded my mind since I had been taught that these areas were private—never to be touched, shown, or talked about. Later, I would be falsely accused of violating my own brother's privacy.

On one particular day, I was in a pair of jeans with a T-shirt and sneakers on. It was late spring or early summer, the sky was overcast and gray, and it began to rain. Ann had given me the punishment of moving large rocks, dozens of them, from one pile to another pile. I didn't know where the next pile would go, but Ann would come out in her raincoat and tell me. There was no indication when the punishment would be done. I was soaked to the bone with dirt and grime on my face and all over my clothes. I was cold and hungry. The punishment didn't make sense to me; it never did. It never seemed to fit the "crime." I was 12—what had I done that could be so bad? I had come to America, the land of the free, or so I thought. Ann believed in corporal punishment, and I hated her for it. She was so cold. I wondered if the rest of my childhood would be this miserable. I planned my next move carefully. I would run away for good.

After two or three hours, Ann told me I was finished. My whole body was sore, my feet throbbing as I walked up to the steps that led into the house. I refused to rush or show any emotion. As I walked past my brother and sister, I smiled inside. They looked like they knew my pain. I took a long shower (alone!), and when I went to bed, I cried into my pillow. I was so hurt inside and had no one to tell. I cried tears of anger, frustration, and pain, but I also cried about feeling so alone and unloved. That hurt the most.

I had made a few attempts to escape the home life that was so depressing and upsetting to me. My mind had the lone thought to be noticed by my parents. In reality, there were walls of silence that remained ever present. The logic was simple to me. If I was not wanted, why should I remain there?

One of my favorite memories was when we visited my grandparents on my adoptive father's side. We always went on Easter Sunday, which was a special occasion with hearty laughter and a lot of activity. I remember my grandmother laboring in the kitchen. She had a beaming smile and a gentle nature. When she got involved in a discussion, it became animated. Everything had to be proper for Granny: "If it is worth doing, then do it superbly the first time," was the motto she lived by. She always slipped me some honey ham or a hot roll, and I had the final say on the veggie dip to ensure its quality.

Over the years, my sister and I took turns sleeping over at Granny's for a weekend. In the morning, I liked to come downstairs and play the piano. I remember my grandmother's encouragement and support as I composed pieces of music. She always thought I should take lessons. Another fond memory was taking walks around the community. Once, we even broke out the tennis rackets and hit the ball around for a while. There was also a pool, and I spent many hours running and jumping into it.

Grampy was a soft-spoken man who gave the greatest hugs. He always asked me if I was okay. "How is school going? Are you playing soccer this year?" It felt like he was genuinely interested. He smoked a pipe, so his sweaters and car had a smoky scent to them. He liked sitting on the leather sofa reading books about sailboats and golfing legends. He had a putter in the basement and taught me how to hit the ball just right. I recall the times Grampy put his hand around Granny's waist and placed a kiss on her cheek while she was cooking. It seemed like they were very much in love after many years of marriage. I had never seen this kind of tenderness anywhere before.

One time the three of us took the train to a baseball game in the city. At an outdoor market, we sampled foods I had never imagined. We sat by third base at the game, and I yelled to the left fielder, Troy, who bore my adopted name.

I miss my paternal grandparents because of the unconditional love and genuine interest they had for us. They never tired of us. I would like to hear their lifetime of stories and shared experiences; I am sure I would glean a lot from the wisdom of their years.

After five years of homeschooling, my parents decided to enroll me in a small, private Christian school. My mother and I met with the principal, who was the pastor of the church that sponsored the school. Pastor Masters was warm and friendly and assured me I would have no problem fitting in. My main interest was the soccer field, and I was sold.

I felt very self-conscious the first few weeks as the new kid. Most of the others had been in school together for a while, but I did my best to get along with everyone and respect my teacher. My good manners went a long way, and I had a slight advantage in reading, writing, and comprehension. I was intimidated by one boy who was referred to as "the brain" (there's always one), but I discovered I could make others laugh and put them at ease. I could also be encouraging if someone was being challenged or having a tough time.

At this new school, I drew the attention of a few girls. Two sisters were constantly poking fun at me and making jokes. This was something new to me, and I was unsure how to respond. I was shy and quiet at times, especially when it came to being in a large group setting (there were 20 others). The playground at recess was challenging for me. I had so many options. Where did I belong? Where could I play or not play? Did older kids hang out with older kids? I didn't know the "rules of the game." Everyone looked like they were having fun, but most of the time I sat off to the side, alone, in the sun. In solitude, it was possible to watch everyone. Thus, I became an observer.

One girl named Anna had been watching me for quite some time. I had never even noticed her. She dressed simply, not like the other girls who wore bright, colorful, stylish clothes. We began to chat a little while we ate lunch and decided to be friends, meeting daily on the playground to talk. She thought I was funny and found out that our fathers worked for the same company. She said she would try to play soccer, even though she often wore long denim skirts and sandals. Soon after, she started writing notes to me. We were "in love" at the age of 12. Anna and I often sat in the bark mulch under the empty seesaw and looked into each other's eyes, both cracking up laughing. One day after school, she moved in for a kiss. People were rushing around getting ready to leave school, but I felt her little lips touch my cheek and her long eyelashes brush my skin. I turned to look, and she was running off giggling and blushing. "Bye-bye," she called as she hopped into her parents' waiting van. I barely got to wave, yet I knew there was a smile on my face.

Alice was the mean girl. She was taller than I and extremely hardheaded. She always batted her eyes and snickered as I walked by. I wish I had understood what she was thinking or had felt comfortable enough to ask someone, but my mother had no compassion and I was not comfortable with any of the staff or students. I think it was jealousy that got the last word in the end. You see, two other girls, Melissa and Melanie, were teasing me about Anna. They said she wasn't cool enough or pretty enough. That just made me like Anna even more, which apparently bothered Alice. She spread rumors of Anna kissing other boys and my sending notes to Alice, but these allegations proved to be false.

What pushed Alice over the edge was when I gave Anna a necklace, and Alice turned even colder and meaner. She no longer looked in my direction or acknowledged my presence. As the school year was ending, my mother received a phone call from the principal, Pastor Masters, and I was called to his office, bewildered. While I waited for my mother, I became nervous about what I could have done to deserve this meeting. As it turned out, I was being expelled from the school. Much to my mother's dismay and my surprise, Alice had accused me of threatening to rape her. My head was swirling with questions, but we were expected to leave quietly. My mother was so sick and so upset that she could not be in my presence. I was confused. I did not even comprehend the concept of sexual intercourse. We hadn't had "the talk"—how could I understand rape? I didn't understand why Alice would say such a thing, and I thought of tenderhearted Anna and our unblemished friendship. My heart ached, and again I cried in solitude.

Chapter 3
DAMAGED GOODS

I recall the months leading up to my removal from our home when I was 13 years old. It must have appeared as though I was unraveling or falling apart—puberty had hit in the form of a wet dream, or nocturnal emission. I soon realized I could manipulate my sex organ for pleasure, and I began masturbating at the age of 13. When my father and I had a short version of "the talk," he did not explain any of this to me but did say it was normal and private. That was the extent of sex education for me. It would be left to me to learn what sex and sexuality was all about. As all this was happening, I was also seeing a psychologist, but he was not aware of my past abuse or trauma. No one knew about the cozy family showers. Now I wish I had shared that information, as things might be very different today. But I kept my secrets to myself. From the time I met my adoptive family, sex and anything to do with it were deemed dirty or illicit.

At the same time, my adoptive parents shared with my counselor that there had been some abuse in my early years. I was not sure where my parents stood on this, and I did not know if they knew the extent or details. So much was left unsaid, and nothing was discussed. I felt from early on that I had to fend for myself; no other person could understand me or what I had been through. I had to learn how to live my life. Throughout the years, this sense of self-reliance would be ingrained in me and would, in turn, keep people away from me.

I was being homeschooled again since the attempt to send me to a small, private school had failed miserably. I did my best to rebel even though some of the work was interesting. I spent hours and weekends in solitude, countless hours of hard labor, or long periods locked in my room. No hope was on the horizon. When I was allowed out, I tried shoplifting. One time, Ann's hand got in the way, and that was it. I guess I was screaming for attention. That did not go well as her arm got bruised in the process.

I also tried stealing Ann's van. The psychotherapy didn't seem to be working, and I wondered if any parenting skills or family therapy would have helped with the lack of communication in the home. None of the events were ever processed with my family, and I never felt any support or compassion. I was alone. So I upped the stakes and started lighting small fires in the backyard, wondering if anyone would notice them and ask *why* I was behaving that way.

One day the four of us, Ann and the kids, went to our great-grandmother's cottage. It was a beautiful day, and Ann chose this time to punish me by restricting me from swimming. I could not even set foot on the deck. I think it would have been better to stay home with a sitter. Nana was surprised by all this as she saw me sulking. I peered out the window for a while, my heart in the dumps, and began to formulate a plan with a dual purpose. I would exact revenge on Ann, if that was possible, and, in my mind, escape forever.

I found my mother's purse and took all the cash and change as well as her van keys. I also took Nana's money with some hesitance. Tiptoeing out of the cottage, I looked over my shoulder one last time before slipping into Ann's van. I had watched her start it before, and now I shifted the gears and rolled out of Nana's driveway, driving a vehicle for the first time at 13½ years old. The dirt road out to the main road was a long, winding one, about a mile long. I made my way to the highway and to the mall where I had some Chinese food for dinner and then played in the arcade for hours, cashing in 20s for change. Once I was bored, I hopped back into the van and headed into the city. I calmly passed Tyngsboro and Medford and got on a ramp. Outside the city, I clipped a Jersey barrier doing 50 miles per hour. The van flipped over three or four lanes in rush hour traffic. When it finally stopped rolling, I took off my seatbelt and started running toward the city on the side of a ramp. There was not a single scratch on me. My dad, looking tired and angry, picked me up later somewhere in Boston. I was wondering if anyone noticed I had been gone for about 10 hours and when the police might start looking for me. My mind pictured a worried mother or grandmother in tears embracing me, but that never happened.

This was the tipping point for my mother. She was officially having a nervous breakdown. Today, she would have been hospitalized, but then it meant I could have no communication with her for about two weeks. I was crushed. The silent treatment was the worst. So I did what I knew best. I slipped out the door one quiet afternoon, disappeared into the woods with the clothes on my back, and was gone for three days. When the police picked me up, they took me to a psychiatric hospital for children, where I remained throughout the holidays. With no visits like all the other children and no Christmas gifts or cards, I felt like a caged animal. The doors were locked all the time. I wondered why no one understood my desire to be free like a bird.

I remained at the hospital for a month or so, watching the lights and decorations go up and come down. There were many nights I cried myself to sleep. I refused recreation time and food as a silent protest, and then I strung up a sheet over a door and tried to hang myself. My mind was in a dark, hopeless place. I was miserable, and I let the world know. When a staff member pushed me from behind, I snapped. All my anger and rage boiled over. I screamed at the top of my lungs, shouting obscenities at this man, and then I went for his throat. As my nails penetrated his skin, the blood trickled down my hands. As a result of this event, they labeled me the "crazy kid." People did not know what to do with me, and I enjoyed that in some strange way. They never had, and I figured no one ever would.

A couple days later, I was placed at a program in the suburbs. I found myself uncomfortable around these boys with "issues," and since a lot of them were bigger and stronger, there was a testing period. Because there was constant noise, I had a hard time sleeping. We had to attend groups to address the cycles of abuse and acting out, and then we watched the female evening staff—mostly in their 20s—come in with tight, revealing shirts, short-shorts, and lots of makeup, perfume, and hair spray. This was very confusing.

I confided in a man who worked third shift. If we behaved, he said he would make pots of coffee and we could stay up late and watch horror movies. I often butted heads with other staff members and got physically restrained, but I did make one friend. One night we snuck out the window and took a car, only to have 10 police cruisers chase us through four towns an hour later. Our car was blocked in a cul-de-sac, and we did not reveal our names, which resulted in an overnight stay in jail. There were four charges added to my juvenile record, and I had a 30-day stay in the youth detention center. I became accustomed to the routine and the harshness of being locked up. The structure was oppressive, and 30 days felt like an eternity, but I finally received news that I would soon be transferred to a retreat in the Berkshires. I wondered if I would ever see my brother and sister again.

In the fall of 1999, I was under lock and key in the Berkshires and feeling like a trapped animal. At the age of 15, I was someone who couldn't be trusted and couldn't make decisions on my own. That all seemed so fitting since I couldn't remember the last time I'd had guidance. The ride there had seemed like forever, and there was no welcome party when we drove up to the Children's Secure Unit. I hadn't seen or heard from any family members in more than a year. Was I being punished or reformed, or was I losing touch with life itself? Why did my parents adopt me?

It took a lot to look at this imposing building without disdain, and I decided not to cooperate. Where would cooperating get me? The staff made things as difficult for me as they could, and I spent the next three months in complete boredom, losing brain function, initiative, and motivation. I learned that there were professionals who dealt with kids like me for a living and that they were always ready with another plan. Once they saw I refused to comply, we moved on to plans B, C, and D. Sooner or later, they packed me up and moved me along. It was self-sabotage, and I was a mess inside, believing that no one loved me and I could not be fixed. I was hurting so bad, but there wasn't a living soul I could call, talk to, or relate to.

I remember a Laotian boy about my age who was also hurting. His eyes were deep pools of sadness, and his body bore scars, burns, and cuts. I often wondered how his heart looked. One night he offered me a bowl of spicy Asian noodles, and we had a bond from then on. He didn't speak English, and I didn't have anyone to speak to. When my life became unbearable, he gave me one thread of human contact.

One day I was up for reevaluation but didn't know why. I put on my best game face and tried not to fidget at a large wooden table. My JPPO (juvenile probation and parole officer), a psychiatrist, a case manager, and the residential advisor were all there, but no family, of course. They established that because I had a myriad of problems, long-term placement was best suited for me. Besides, where else would they put a minor?

I was considered and approved for yet another placement: Riverview School in Vermont. Whenever I faced a lengthy waiting process, I went stir-crazy with nowhere to go, no vacation, and no ability to go home on leave. I just wanted to find a place where I fit in, where I could find some semblance of peace, normalcy, and actual life. Riverview lasted eight months. There was always the adjustment phase and a pecking order to navigate. As the young, skinny Costa Rican kid, I was at the bottom of that pecking order until the others saw me play soccer, and then I rose quite quickly to the level of the athletes' clique. There were also genuine staff members who cared about the work they had chosen—it was more than just a job with a paycheck. I noticed that they viewed us as individuals who needed varying degrees of help, support, and treatment.

For the first time ever, I learned consistency and true respect. I had the same teacher and teacher's aide all year. The teacher's aide was my favorite staff member. Her name was Shanta, an immigrant from India who was constantly surprising us with treats. We all loved them since most of us had lived away from home for quite some time. The whole class grew very fond of her even though she demanded the strictest level of respect for our elders, teachers, coaches, and residential staff. One day we went swimming and canoeing, and I still remember the look on Shanta's face as I rocked our canoe and tipped it over. It never occurred to me that she might not be able to swim, but she received my joking around with warmth and good humor.

I grew up loving soccer. It was one of my strong connections with Costa Rica. It was a common language that many people understood and were passionate about. On the field, I was fast, bold, and creative. I felt very alive. My teammates often gave me encouraging words, and by the second season, I was elected co-captain. We enjoyed great cohesion as a team and carried that over to the dorms and classes. At Riverview, we understandably spent a lot of time outdoors biking, swimming, camping, skiing, and more. The outdoors was our medication and therapy. What a novel idea! Capitalize on individual strengths and healthy activities instead of people's weaknesses and problems, and don't use drugs to mask their symptoms. This was the first time I saw people growing and being happy instead of remaining depressed, anxious, and often suicidal. The students there were productive in school and successful in other activities. Marc, my case manager, often said, "Grab a water bottle and your bike, kid; let's have a talk."

I really looked up to Ed, a staff member who was assigned as my "big brother." Ed was a giant of a man at 6 feet 6 inches tall and

280 pounds of muscle, with a big heart and gentle demeanor. I don't remember him ever raising his voice, but we always listened and did what he asked. Football was his game. One time he took a few of us to the New York Giants training camp (Who does that?). We had the privilege of watching professional football players train on the field. I later learned that Ed was supposed to play for the Giants when he got out of college, but an injury sidelined him. Wherever he is today, I hope to thank him for the enormous, positive impact he had on my life—the love and patience he showed a young man starved of these invaluable feelings for so long meant the world to me.

My overall experience at Riverview was positive, and I was blessed with several opportunities I still appreciate today. Toward the end of my stay there, I was selected along with five other boys to take a three-week cross-country survival experience in the Grand Canyon. Most of us had never left our neighborhoods or placements. We stopped at Lake Powell in Utah and went through Colorado and New Mexico. The trip went by so fast, like a blur, yet I gained a greater appreciation for nature and our resourcefulness.

In fall 2001, high school for me was beginning to wind down. After packing up, I once again felt very uncertain about my future. I had lived with this element of the unknown for so long that you would think I would be used to it, but I was still full of fear and had no home base at age 17. I was in a place called the West House for teens to transition out of the system after high school, yet I had nowhere to go after that. I gradually began to fit in and became more comfortable, but there was usually friction between staff and clients. I gravitated toward a group who listened to music, or I just spent time alone. I was introduced to Islam and considered converting. But when I had plans to attend a local mosque, the events that occurred in September 2001 changed my position on this religion of "peace."

Due to the combination of my learning disabilities and behavioral issues, the powers that be decided to send me to an alternative school. They also decided that a couple of counseling sessions a month might fix me. I struggled to answer question after question that I simply did not have answers to. I was frustrated, angry, and bitter inside that my adoptive parents would not even give me a chance to go back home and prove myself. The sinking feeling in the pit of my stomach was real. I had no family, never had, and never would again. I would turn 18, the system would kick me out, and I would be all alone without any family or support. Here are some of the questions that constantly swirled around in my head: Why did my adoptive parents uproot me? Why did they bring me here only to abandon me? What about my siblings? Were they practically perfect in every way? Did they measure up to Ann's standards? Did they make the grade? Where did my adoptive father fit in?

I reluctantly started my new school. I did well there except for the distraction of a girl named Janelle. She caused a lot of anxiety for me and everyone she met. She was toxic. I was unable, or unwilling, to play soccer during my last year of high school since the school was too small and the town had a young junior varsity team that was just not my speed. So I got my first part-time job. I laid low for the first few months. I don't remember exactly what my undoing was, but I do admit I liked to push the limits. I had a rebellious spirit and a sense of hopelessness—a recipe for disaster. An overwhelming sense of sadness led up to the holiday season, and as Thanksgiving approached, I soon realized I was the only person with nowhere to go for the holiday. A staff member, John, took me to his family gathering, and we had a great meal, but I was devastated by the sense of loss and loneliness. That cut deeper and deeper inside me with each holiday and birthday that passed. Soon, I found myself in front of a judge trying to excuse my lack of cooperation again. I was on the move.

This time, I barely got into a place that was willing to take me. It was as if I had reached the end of the road. The alternative was a youth detention center. By my account, even through running away, a suicide attempt, fist fights, and high-speed police chases, God had His hand on me. He always had a purpose and a plan. God never wastes anything, either. He uses everything in our lives for some reason.

Once again, my future was uncertain. It was up in the air where I would go and what I would do when I turned 18. I decided to take the wheel and attempt to direct the course of my life.

It still amazes me to think of all I went through alone. Now I know there was a powerful and loving God watching over me during all those times. He was contending for my life, heart, love, and overall well-being. That sounds like grace, doesn't it?

Chapter 4

TOO MANY MISTAKES

I have always respected our nation's armed forces. There was something about watching military parades as a child that captivated me. I'm sure part of it was all the fanfare, but I loved the crisp uniforms, the oiled guns, and the curt salutes. The medals, ribbons, and ranks also impressed me. Perhaps a man could prove himself by joining the military. These thoughts, along with the tragedy of 9/11, led to my decision to inquire about enlisting. Due to my troubled youth, joining the military was not a sure thing. I had a record with the law, and there was no way around that. Still, exceptions were made, and I signed my life away a month after my 18th birthday. I was put on a waitlist and then scheduled to leave about six months later, shipping out for basic combat training the following spring.

Meanwhile, I met a girl named Sarah, and we began to date. From the beginning, our relationship revolved around sex, which was a first for me. I know I was probably not for her, but I was a healthy, Latino man hungry for attention, affection, and any kind of gratification, so I did not complain. I equated sex with love and belonging. Let there be no mistake, I had engaged in carnal, sexual acts before, but not the entire time during a relationship.

I didn't even know where I would be living, so I decided to enroll in the Job Corps while waiting for basic training. This decision put some separation between Sarah and me since the Job Corp's training center was in Tremont, a good distance from where she lived.

Over the summer, I volunteered to work on a sailboat. The owner was a man who knew of the boys' home where I had been placed. The job paid very well, and I later learned that he was a self-made millionaire. Once the work was done, he invited me to stay overnight on the boat and gave me a crash course in sailing and navigation the following day. After supper, we smoked some weed, and he asked if I wanted a drink. My experience with alcohol was limited, but of course I said sure—a foolish decision. A rocking boat is probably not the best place to try vodka for the first time. My stomach churned while this slime ball guy told me to loosen up and go with it. Fortunately, I threw up all over the cabin, and that killed the mood. Regretful and disgusted, I left the next morning after refusing his offer to sail down to the Caribbean from island to island, through the Panama Canal, and back to San Diego. Believe me, I actually think I made a good choice.

I arrived at the Job Corps in Tremont in late fall and planned to enroll in a construction course. There was an orientation of new students, and I learned it was common to hook up with someone in your group. That is when I met Alley. We dated through the winter and became intimate, of course. Neither of us had even considered using protection of any kind, so when Alley became pregnant, it was not a surprise to either of us. Remember, I equated sex with love. Because we were determined to keep the child, we told Alley's mother she was pregnant. Her mother tried not to react strongly and remained uninvolved.

We knew there would be challenges ahead, and soon we were put to the test. I had plans with the military I had to follow, and Alley knew about that, but I hoped I could return and be part of the baby's life. Accusations of infidelity arose and drove a wedge between us. A month later, we spent our last weekend together, making promises of a future life together. It was as if the very fabric of our lives and time were slipping away with my impending departure. Two days later, I boarded a plane to the South for boot camp, an experience that would be both an intense and exciting period of my life. I witnessed what it was like to be stripped of one's individualism and transformed into a valuable asset of a team.

Twelve weeks later, I graduated. My friend's mother, Marcy, was there because no one else would come. I was so proud that I could send her money for airfare. We spent the day together, and I heard the words I longed to hear: "I am so proud of you!" It had been 10 years or more since I had heard those words, especially with any energy and enthusiasm. I cherished that moment, tucking it away to replay it repeatedly.

My first set of orders arrived for me to report to my permanent duty station. Alley had been writing to me all during the pregnancy, and I treasured the sonograms she sent me. Making sure to call once a week, I did the best I could to show support. I felt like life was okay for the first time since my childhood. I had money in the bank, and I was learning valuable skills and training. There were options and opportunities coming up for me. I was considering training for Special Forces, the best of the best, the "Tip of the Spear." I knew in my heart that I had what it took to excel despite all odds. My mind pondered going overseas to war. Would I survive? At what cost? There was a small part of me that was fearful, afraid to die.

Some of my training experiences reminded me of my childhood home. On one particular day, the smell of rain was in the air, and I didn't want to be out there. Up the line, just around the curve of the road, the platoon leader stopped. What now? We all followed suit and stopped in our tracks. A hand signal went out for two scouts to come forward, followed by a second signal to drop to the ground. Something was about to happen. My whole body was tense, and my mind went into overdrive. I scanned the wood line on both sides of the road. Nothing.

It was late afternoon, and the sun was fading fast. The cold, chilling rain pelted down on my face and neck. I gazed down at the assault rifle in my hands, hoping I could still shoot it if I needed to. Wet steel was worse than wet skin. Someone scurried by toward the rear of the column. I heard whispers. Five minutes later, we were on the move again and reached our destination without incident.

Later, at about two a.m., my eyes wanted to close. I was exhausted. We could have no fires tonight since we were in hostile territory. My boots and socks were soaked through, and my briefs clung to my shivering body. I heard the rain on the leaves overhead, but it did not remind me of the rain forest in Costa Rica. It was warm there. I fell asleep for a while but was abruptly awakened by the shrill sound of a command. "Time to move!" No break, no sustenance. How long could this go on? "Time to go! Snap to!" I almost slipped and fell on a tree root but trudged on. The rain slanted from side to side, and it was muddy now. I hoped we could make it out of these godforsaken woods.

After a while, the letters from Alley stopped coming. Whenever I called, she never seemed to be around or available. It hit me hard that our relationship was over. I was crushed that someone I trusted and cared about had betrayed me.

My mentality changed with the season and the new surroundings. I welcomed the attention of another woman who was stationed near my barracks. I looked forward to the possibility of being shipped overseas. My unit had a detachment in Italy, and we were about to be deployed. I tasted freedom and liked the prospect of leaving everything behind. A fellow soldier and I shared our hopes and dreams. We had about six months of training left before we could ask for leave. Part of me wanted to see my newborn daughter, and then there was the girl back home who was all about sex. In the face of uncertainty, I was looking for the familiar. I wanted to go home, but I didn't have one.

One day while preparing for inspection, a soldier I had previously had a conflict with joined my unit. I could feel his eyes glaring at the back of my head, but I let it go and walked away. Our company was to leave for Airborne Jump School in a week, so our mindset was that this was an important opportunity to advance toward our military goals. Nothing could jeopardize that. Unfortunately, the other soldier did not agree and kicked me as hard as he could in the back. I spun around and grabbed him by the neck, pummeling him until he needed medical attention. My superiors were furious, and there was talk of formal charges. The thought of spending time in a military prison during a war was more than I could take after a break from a life of institutions. So during the night, I quietly packed and ran. Within 24 hours, I was near my so-called hometown. I lied to people who knew me and told them I had received an early leave, deciding to crash at a friend's house and get a job. My next call was to "that girl," Sarah, and our sex life ramped back up.

A couple months later, I was arrested for two misdemeanors, and once I was processed, the military placed a detainer on me. They flew me to Kentucky to be discharged. My inappropriate behaviors could have resulted in a reduction in pay and less leave time, but I could also have received prison time. Had I only faced the situation head-on and not run to escape, my life might be very different today.

While I did take a bus home where "that girl" was waiting for me, I could not forget about my daughter. I had begun to associate seasons in nature with parts of my life. Fall almost always brought about change. Winter was a contemplative time for me. Spring and summer usually brought joy and happy memories.

My friend's mother, Marcy, was getting tired of housing a bunch of kids, and I struck out to find an affordable place to live. I ended up changing jobs and living with Sarah and her parents for a couple of months. Her parents made ground rules, and we trampled, broke, and defied every one of them, disrespecting her parents completely.

I bounced to yet another job, and afterward yet another arrest. So I was stuck at my girlfriend's house for the winter. I got her car towed, which impressed her parents even more. Finally, after finding another job, I did get a decent apartment—my first place. Sarah and I decorated it, furnished it, did drugs, and drank. That was the last time for me because I never liked feeling out of control.

Chapter 5

THE VESSEL BEGINS TO CRACK
(THE UNDERBELLY IS UGLY)

There was a sense of normalcy to the routine that had become my life. I felt that since I had a stable job, I should at least make the effort to remain stable. Sarah wanted to take a break for a while to see other people, news that continued to nag at my heart. She had just told me she was pregnant with our child, and I could not shake the feeling that I might lose her and my unborn child. This situation seemed to fit my life pattern. People came into my life, I started to care about them, and then they left.

Sarah suffered from severe mood swings, depression, and panic attacks, which only became worse as her hormones became impacted by pregnancy. I was trying to hold it all together, and after some encouraging words from a friend, I committed to becoming more responsible. Any money I had left over after expenses I scrupulously saved for diapers and a couple of toys. I also searched for a more spacious apartment to live in. There were times when I sought counsel from Sarah's mother, with whom I had a healthy, courteous relationship. I also dropped by Sarah's sister's place and helped her do laundry since she had a five-year-old son who thought of me as his uncle. I was often entrusted with his care on the weekends or whenever his parents wanted a night out. All this was motivated by my desire to have the family or support system I had always lacked. I realized that as time went on, the prospect of having a newborn began to really sink in.

It had been a couple of weeks since Sarah and I had seen each other or even talked on the phone. It seemed like there was a giant wall of silence between us. I had been trying to make sense of it all, but at best, I was confused. Sarah had suffered serious mental and emotional turmoil prior to the pregnancy, so I was concerned about how the hormones might impact her. I knew from her sister and other friends that she had come from a very dark place, and I wanted to do anything I could to support her. On one occasion, I was visiting her at her parents' home, and she excused herself to go to the bathroom. She had been gone a while when I saw a worried look creep over her mother's face. I went to the bathroom, and all I could hear were sobs and cries. Sarah said she didn't know if she would be better off alive or dead, and I realized that my pregnant girlfriend was threatening suicide. She told me she had a bunch of sleeping pills in her hand. I pleaded with her not to take them but to give us a chance to talk things out. She finally gave in and opened the door. I flushed the pills down the toilet. I did my best to comfort her, but my mind was filled with fear and doubt. I called her sister to see if she had any insight, but she said that, unfortunately, this was quite typical. She didn't know if it was a ploy for attention or a true desire to end her life. I emptied the rest of the bottle and saw that it was a sleep aid. After Sarah lay down on the couch, she was unable to talk about the situation and drifted off to sleep.

On another occasion, Sarah broke down sobbing while we were in the car. She was driving, and as we reached the top of a very large, familiar hill, she sped the car up to a dangerously high speed, more than 70 miles per hour. Out of the corner of my eye, I could see she was relatively calm. She had been quite sullen for the last few hours, and I should have known something was wrong when she didn't slow down sooner. I heard her mumble, "I want it all to end." The car started to veer to the left side of the road. I nudged her leg off the gas pedal, and she began to scream. Then I pulled the emergency brake. After we slid sideways into the woods, I sat in disbelief, wondering what could possibly be next. My mind begged an unanswerable question: What is wrong with this girl? Sarah burst into tears and I held her, wondering if it was all an act for attention or if I would ever get any answers. I took her home, hugged her to tell her that I cared, and collapsed at my home with tears in my eyes.

One of the few people I could turn to in a time of need was Marcy. In my eyes, she was a wonderful woman, the closest to a mother I had ever experienced. There were so many reasons I appreciated her, including her willingness to attend my boot camp graduation ceremony. She lived five minutes down the road and told me I could drop by anytime. The fact that she had a stable full of majestic, beautiful, powerful horses may have had something to do with my fondness for her property, but I also loved her as a person. Marcy and I always took the time to catch up with each other over a cup of coffee, and then we would make our way out to the barn. We could hear and smell the amazing animals far off in the distance. Marcy announced her presence to the horses as we unlocked the big, heavy wooden doors, and the horses snorted and neighed in response. We would lead them one by one out to the paddock and then clean out the stables. I watched closely as Marcy spoke to the horses, chuckling as they vied for her attention, almost like young children. She patted their heads and threw out fresh hay for them to eat. I have carried these precious moments in my heart all these years, which has helped me keep hope and love alive. They are simple moments, frozen in time, undisturbed by anything else that has taken place.

Marcy did not always tell me what I wanted to hear. She gently shared that all the confusion I was experiencing with my girlfriend could simply be a phase she was going through. But she had also seen a lot of life and was honest about its realities. It was sobering to hear that everything might not work out after all. Marcy advised me to focus on work and keep planning and saving for the future, whatever that might be.

Numerous times I took a long walk by myself, trying to figure out life. It also became a habit to drive a few miles after work at night since it was the closest I could get to finding a semblance of peace. As I turned in one night, I noticed how badly my small studio apartment needed cleaning. I had my last smoke, thought about the work week and the repairs my car would soon need, and settled on the fact that there was no food in the refrigerator. My choice was food or gas, and I needed gas to get to work.

I awoke Monday morning before the alarm on my cell phone went off. I relished the few moments I had and enjoyed a smoke. I had been meaning to quit this persisting, unhealthy habit. It would be tough, but I thought about the money it would save and the provision it would represent for the two people in my life. So I decided to quit, just not today.

As I pulled on my work boots, I wondered how Sarah was doing. My cell phone rang just as I reached for it. The call was from my co-worker, who was also Sarah's brother-in-law. He wanted to know if I was meeting him at his place or if he was picking me up. I told him I would be at his place in a few minutes and then made my way down the stairs and to the curb. My car door was locked with the keys inside. I could not believe this blunder. I had thought of myself as sharp, someone with his wits about him. I decided it was best to call for a ride and not waste time.

My ride made his usual stop at the gas station, and I worried as I purchased my coffee and muffin. Would I have enough money to get to work and back for the week? What about food, gas, and cigarettes? I knew I could count on my friend for a couple of these necessities, but not everything. These questions swirled in my mind all the way to

THE VESSEL BEGINS TO CRACK (THE UNDERBELLY IS UGLY)

work. Once we got there, we went right to work and didn't stop until noon. I went for the lunch run to a local sandwich shop, still feeling worried. Finally, I decided to give my parents a call. This would be a first for me to ask for money or any kind of help. My parents had not provided any kind of support for years (maybe six or seven). The rings on the phone line seemed to be separated by a slow, dreadful silence, and I think I stopped breathing waiting for someone to answer the phone. My mother finally answered. I didn't see the point in making small talk since we truly had nothing to discuss, so I explained my current situation. Despite my hard work, I had to decide between food, rent, or gas to commute to work. In my mind, this was a last resort. My mother still had a sharp, cold, indifferent tone to her voice. She informed me she would think it over and discuss it with my father. I promised I would pay it back since I was due for a raise in a couple of months.

As I returned to work, my palms were sweaty, and my stomach churned. It was hard to even imagine what it would take to finally gain my parents' approval and measure up to any of their standards they had silently imposed on me over the years. I was striving to show my parents and the world that I had at least *some* worth. In my mind, I was becoming responsible. I had a job with decent pay, a car that ran, an attractive girlfriend, and a future in mind.

I thought about all the promotional offers I had received in my email account, usually filtered as spam. There was a job offering in the Gulf of Mexico that seemed to have my name on it. The starting pay was nearly triple what I was currently making. Maybe I should try that and leave everything and everyone behind. Then, there was the option to reenlist in the Army.

I brushed some of the grime off me as I got into my friend's car, and we rode back home in silence. As he dropped me off, I mentioned I was supposed to look at an apartment in a couple of hours. He said it would be okay if I stopped by his house for supper. We had helped each other out a lot over the last year. This 30-year-old man, an unmotivated individual who expected the world to revolve around him, was the closest I had to an uncle or older brother. I took my time showering and then went to see my landlord about either getting a loan or getting my security deposit back. He was interested in fixing up the rundown car I kept on his property. Perhaps that had some value. The man hemmed and hawed for a few minutes as we stood outside. I conveyed my intention to move out and my need for money. He would not be able to give me the deposit until the following week. We parted ways, and I headed toward my friend's place, as my appointment to see another apartment was not for another hour.

My mind attempted to juggle and sort out all the new developments. It felt like things were in one sense coming together but at the same time falling apart. There seemed to be so little I could do to influence or control the very circumstances that constituted my life, my future, and my own livelihood. This had presented a challenge for me as far back as I could remember. Life was, after all, about finding one's own destiny, right? Either way, I would have to fend for myself in the long run. I felt I had never been able to rely on someone else.

I made sure to take my cell phone with me as well as directions to the apartment, feeling a sense of anticipation as I settled into my car and drove down the road. I was turning over in my head and heart the implications of a new place to live, a fairly new job, and a child on the way. Sarah and I had even talked of marriage down the road, although we had received some heady counseling from her pastor regarding such a life-altering decision.

I lit a cigarette as I thought about how difficult the last six months had been for Sarah and me, all the way back to my discharge from the army the previous fall. When I returned, I felt like an interruption in people's lives rather than being welcomed back or having my service acknowledged. Sarah seemed uncomfortable when I walked into the room and found her on the phone. She fidgeted and grew silent. Sometimes she was speaking in a hushed tone and then awkwardly hung up. I wondered what the secrecy was all about until I began hearing rumors that she was cheating, but I pushed the thought out of my mind. I did not want to consider the possibility. I wanted to trust her, or someone—anyone. I wanted to give her the benefit of the doubt. Since we were together and constantly having sex, I did not pick up on any of the clues around me. It took her sister pulling me aside for the truth to sink in. My girlfriend was not who I thought she was. Learning that hurt me to my core.

When I finally confronted her, she broke down and begged me to stay with her. It was enough of a convincing act for me. I held on to a belief and misplaced trust that we could make it as a couple and eventually a family, but there was something else going on. Our recent break had shaken me to the core. I wanted to believe that by proving myself as a man who could provide for my family, everything else would fall into place.

That night as I passed Sarah's sister-in-law's apartment, I saw Sarah's car in the driveway. I thought this was odd since she told me she was working. So I decided to turn around and stop by. I had to park down the street in a lot adjacent to the community church I had visited a handful of times with Sarah. It was a warm evening with just a hint of a breeze, and the apartment seemed quieter than usual as I approached. There was a bustle of activity in the dirt lot. Sarah's brother was working on a car with a guy I had run into a while back when he had been babysitting with Sarah and drinking beers. When I showed up, he became angry. He looked surprised as I walked up, but I looked back calmly and shook his hand. I really did want to move on.

I made my way to Sarah's sister-in-law's apartment and up the long stairs. I was greeted by the laughter and screaming of four or five children. Sarah answered the door, looking annoyed, and I followed her into the kitchen to say hello to her sister-in-law, who did not seem to care for me for some reason or other. I was open, calm, and friendly, while they seemed distant and unreceptive. I felt a cringe in my chest as the old, familiar sense of rejection crept in. I was trying very hard to put my best foot forward, but something was definitely not right. There must have been a consensus that I was blind or completely oblivious to what was happening.

I told Sarah I had a surprise for her, and she rolled her eyes. She did not seem to be in the mood for surprises. That should not have been new to me after what we were going through, but I was bubbling inside, wanting to tell her about the apartment. I was going to look at an apartment for us. Things would work out. What could be better? But I didn't get to tell her since her sister-in-law barged in on us. She had an annoying habit of doing that. She suggested that Sarah and I go down to the ice cream parlor to pick up treats for the kids. I jumped at the opportunity. We made our way out to Sarah's car, and I could not help but notice the look on the other guy's face. I still did not register that there was something going on between the two of them. We drove in silence to the ice cream parlor. I tried being humorous, even a little goofy as we bought an array of treats and a milkshake for the two of us. Still, the silence and lack of communication started to bother me. I could hear my own breathing as we made our way back to her sister-in-law's apartment. The world outside the car seemed to slow down a bit, almost as if to wait for us through the sound of the car's engine.

Chapter 6

THE PAST MEETS THE PRESENT

As we rounded the bend, I asked Sarah to pull into the parking lot where I had parked my car. We sat in silence, parked parallel to my car. As I became more frustrated and worried, I decided to ask what was going on. She stumbled around for words and then reaffirmed the need for space between us and some time apart. I thought we had been taking a break but was beginning to wonder to what end. How long would the break be, and what were the terms of this break? All the uncertainty I thought I had left behind was still very present in our relationship. Her face was blank, passive, and almost expressionless. I felt confused. Where had we gone wrong? I anxiously searched my mind, trying to take hold of something, anything.

A minute later, we were on the road again. Less than a mile or so from our destination, we agreed that soon we needed to talk alone to make some sense of all this. As we crossed the bridge and headed down a familiar street, I felt a chill in the air. It seemed like everything was happening in slow motion. I smiled a little and took comfort in the fact that we were on the same road we had been on so many times before. This place held a lot of good memories. Sarah and I had visited this quiet, out-of-the-way place to escape the outside world when we just needed a break. The woods had always been sort of a refuge for me, probably due to my childhood in the rain forest. There was a stream within walking distance, and I had spent hours along it teaching myself photography.

The sunlight streamed through the tall trees. We were surrounded by lush, green bushes and other vegetation, and my window was cracked open to smell the fresh air and sweet scent of wildflowers that were blooming on the forest floor. I tried to brace myself for whatever Sarah had to say, but she remained silent. Finally, I asked her what was wrong. What had I done to deserve the silent treatment? While I glanced down at the cigarette in her hand, she mumbled something. I asked her to repeat herself. She said, "You just don't get it." Emotion began to rise in me because I had long been sent away to special schools, and my parents had abandoned me, but I thought I had proved myself to her and her family. Recently, people had told me I was a quick learner on the job. I felt that people in general thought I was an intelligent, responsible person. Who was she to say I could not grasp something she had never tried to explain? My forehead suddenly felt hot, and my chest was tight. I noticed Sarah's hand slide over, and I felt her cigarette searing my skin as she told me I was stupid. A tidal wave of emotion swept over me.

I was suddenly back in Costa Rica with my father looming over me. His shadow enveloped my small body as I stood still, silent with fear. I blinked as I watched myself take her small frame by the shoulders, intending to calm her and stop her demeaning comments, to settle the madness that had begun minutes earlier. An unfamiliar sense rose around me, and there was a sudden, overwhelming darkness. As the surrounding forest grew darker, I felt like someone was watching us or something was converging on our location. I begged Sarah to calm down, wanting to believe she was the one who was upset, unhinged, out of control like so many times before. Her arm tensed, and again I expected some act of aggression. Her hand balled up around a pen or one of the chopsticks she kept in her console for her hair.

My hand tightened on her shoulders as I pulled her toward me. I was alone again in Costa Rica, miles from home. The sun was setting on the horizon, I had inadequate clothing, and the air was cool. I dreaded the long walk back, wishing for a light or a voice to guide me. I had learned to walk with my eyes almost completely closed because I was so fearful of the darkness beyond the road's edge. My heart sank as it began to rain when I reached home. There in that hut, the drops of rain became very loud, eventually ringing out into a rhythm. I tried not to focus on my father touching me and violating me. There were miles between us and anyone else. Would anyone ever know or care? It hurt so bad and made me angry inside. I never got to talk to my younger siblings about this, or anyone else for that matter.

I wanted to silence my girlfriend now. I wanted her to see who I was. She would see I wasn't stupid. I was not the one to cheat on her. I did have value. My fingers on my left hand were wet, but I barely noticed the blood. I was there in the car with her, though light-years away.

I fell back through time—13, 14, 15 years earlier. Holding my breath, I wanted it to be over. The wooden floorboard smelled musty. I fixed my mind on the head of one solitary nail sticking out from a floorboard. His breathing was strained and heavy. Then a distant separation while I remained on my side, frozen and silent.

Sarah's head dropped forward, her chin resting on her chest. I blinked, sucking in a deep breath. It was horrible! The intense smell of iron was in the air. The car's cabin was stuffy now, and something was wrong, very wrong. My lips quivered as I began to process what was before me. Sarah's hair was matted with blood. Her breathing was shallow and labored. I now saw blood everywhere, including my own hands, but I had no memory of what had just happened.

Tears flooded my eyes. It was too much. My mind wanted to shut down, yet my senses struggled to keep me in the moment. I called out to her and got a whispered response. I got out of the car and almost fell on my face, unsteady with shock. I had to move her to the passenger side to get her to the hospital. My mind drew a blank on any memory of first aid training. Sliding into the driver's seat, I told her we were on the way to the hospital. I was going to get her help.

I promised myself I wouldn't lose her. The car careened off the dirt road onto a back road, swerving and pushing to its limit. We drifted across the road as the car sped up to 60, 70, 80 miles per hour. Three miles went by in a blur. I desperately searched for my new cell phone to call for help, but I came up empty-handed. It would later be verified that the cell phone was indeed in the car during those frantic moments, just inches away, out of sight under the passenger seat. Precious moments came and went. I steadied my hands on the wheel as I tried to map out the shortest route to the nearest hospital. It was going to be close, but I believed we could make it.

My heart was pounding harder and faster in my chest. It was getting harder to breathe. The steering wheel felt slippery, and I noticed a steady flow of blood from my hand. I couldn't remember why I was bleeding. My eyes welled up with tears, and agony coursed through my body. As I glanced over to check on Sarah's condition, I saw a junction in the road. To my hampered recollection, this road was not familiar to me. Confusion and fear began to set in. I reached into the back seat and grabbed a pair of Sarah's scrub pants to put on one of her wounds. She was mumbling something over and over. "I'm sorry, I'm sorry…I love you, I love you…" Her breathing was shallow. I told her she had nothing to be sorry for. She pulled the scrubs off her wound. Confused, I asked her why. The car came dangerously close to the shoulder of the road as I tried to hear her words. I had no idea how fast the car was going or even what road we were on. The next time I looked over, her lifeless eyes were staring through me.

I didn't think it was possible to cry harder. At first, I continued to drive toward where I thought the hospital was, vaguely recognizing the road I was on. Then reality began to set in. I was driving Sarah's car, covered in her blood, and her body was in the passenger seat. Who would ever believe my version of events? As I passed a convenience store, I wondered if I should call for an ambulance, but that led me to the same conclusion. My mind began to operate in a mode not familiar to me. I needed to shut all emotion down and think clearly. Sarah needed a burial, or at least a peaceful resting place. A couple miles later, I noticed a sprawling patch of land that was out of the way. Her body would not be disturbed. I slowly pulled off the road and carried her in my arms. There was wild grass growing all around, and I simply thought this was a natural place. My heart broke again as I watched her stare into the sky. I placed her arms across her chest, and with hope, I checked to see if she had any sign of life. I waited a few agonizing minutes, my heart heavy with sorrow. Kneeling beside her, I spoke quietly to her, my eyes stinging with tears once again. I took the necklace she had on as something to remember her by, knowing I would never see her again. The whole situation was impossible to grasp—she had been here one moment and then was gone the next. I slowly trudged back to the car, my stomach lurching.

I wanted to get as far away as possible from this tragedy, this town, this day, all of it. Pulling back onto the main road, I eventually wound up on the highway. When I realized I was headed north, I took the next exit and headed south.

I tried to collect my thoughts, but I was now at the point of exhaustion and the most anxious I had ever been. The feeling was one of being completely out of control and lost. After lighting a cigarette and throwing it away, I noticed blood from my fingers seeping into the filter. I drove on, hopeless, wanting it all to end. My heart sank as I realized I could not return to my apartment. Now I was destined to be forever on the run, frantically trying to hide to avoid being apprehended. Could all this be left behind? I wanted to push this tragic, painful experience deep inside to be forgotten forever.

My hands gripped the steering wheel tightly as I raced down the highway. I wondered how much gas was in the tank. My mind barely registered the large yellow signs cautioning of a toll up ahead. I began to anxiously wonder what the toll attendant would think as I pulled up with blood on my hands and clothes. Not wanting to be caught and still holding to the belief that I could put as much space between me and the recent events, I sped up and blasted through the narrow opening. I pushed the car faster, and soon the tolls were a tiny speck in my rearview mirror. My mind was starting to completely function again when I noticed a lone vehicle in front of me. I was driving so fast that in a moment, I was upon it and had to swerve not to collide with it. As dusk settled in, I glanced in my rearview mirror. One car was cresting the small hill I had blown over about a mile back. My eyes blinked to register that not only was this the same car I had barely missed hitting, but it had a flashing red light on its dash. This car was gradually gaining ground, and in that moment, the chase was on.

I felt so alone, so far removed from the world I had come to know. I had crossed a big line, and there was no turning back, no explaining. We were the only two vehicles on this road for a while, and then I encountered a dozen cars and traffic. I drove on and on, watching as police cruiser after cruiser joined the pursuit. I had resolved in my heart that I would not be caught. I preferred to die rather than face the consequences. The chase continued for nearly an hour but seemed much longer. Finally, in the end, my car ran out of gas. I was cornered, trapped. A frenzy ensued as dozens of officers converged on the scene, and I was wrestled out of the car at gunpoint. I never had any weapons. As I lay on my stomach, relief flooded me. All I knew to be ceased to exist in that moment as the officers handcuffed me and proceeded to search the car.

Someone examined me, and soon an ambulance arrived and took me to a local hospital. Through my tears and mumbling, I tried to tell the officers and medics I was physically okay. My heart, my very soul cried out in agony as I thought of my now-deceased girlfriend lying on the ground, two states away. She could have used this medical attention two hours ago, but it was too late now. The pain hurt too much to try to settle this within myself. It was too late. It was done. It was irreversible.

Chapter 7
GOD WOULD NEVER WANT ME

That morning was the same as every other morning that week. It was unusual for me, but I had not showered and had barely eaten anything in days. The cuts on my fingers, now stitched up, were healing; I could feel my skin pulling itself together. The rest of me, however, was not. I felt like I would succumb to death at any moment. There was pity in the eyes of some of the guards who checked on me every couple of hours. Others would mumble comments, perhaps threats, under their breath. The same guards slid my food tray under the door and slammed it loudly.

There was some sense of relief when a pair of guards approached my cell with two men in suits who informed me that they were detectives. I was weak and shaken when I held out my hands to be handcuffed. A blast of air from the air conditioner in the hallway gave me a scent of boot leather and aftershave. I fixed my gaze straight down the hallway, and soon we were buzzed into the adjacent port. The escort snapped into action. Handguns were checked out and holstered, and someone made a call on their cell phone. They led me toward an awaiting sedan and asked if I wanted a bulletproof vest. I hesitated for a moment but then mumbled no. My attitude was not exactly optimistic. My mindset was that if I was going to be gunned down, I of all people must have it coming. I braced myself for the inevitable brightness of sunlight as the garage door opened. It was about nine a.m. when we headed out in silence. My eyes soon noticed a nondescript vehicle following us, and I wondered if the windows in the cruiser were bulletproof. Would I feel anything if I was hit by a bullet? I felt a sinking feeling as my mind caught up with a fleeting memory. My victim's father had served as a sniper in Vietnam. I pictured the well-oiled and maintained rifle I had stumbled upon months earlier.

I listened as the detective in the front passenger seat spoke softly into a cell phone. We were on our way, and someone was expecting us. I mused that a few people were probably waiting for me as I sat sandwiched between two men in the back seat. As if on cue, one asked me if I was okay. Yeah, I thought, I was having the ride of my life. After they advised me of my Miranda rights, I began to wonder what was going to happen to me. How long could I be sentenced to prison? Would I survive? The detectives advised me of my legal rights once I engaged them in conversation. I had so many questions that no one seemed to have solid, reliable answers to.

Within an hour, we were driving down familiar streets. We were in the town I had lived in only a week earlier, and soon I was shuffled into a small interview room of a crowded police station. Everyone had very grim looks on their faces, and a tall man I had never seen before entered the room. He quietly commanded everyone's attention and sat down across from me, smiling with a thin folder in his hand.

The next few hours were a blur. They obtained permissions. They photographed my naked body. They conducted a third interview, and people swarmed around the room and the station's hallways. People made multiple phone calls, and just as quickly as this whole process started, it came to a grinding halt. An officer very deliberately and precisely pushed the off button on the tape recorder. I took what felt like my first breath all day. My eyes teared up for the third or fourth time—I'd lost track. I let tears run down my cheeks, and my body shook. The five or six men in the room clenched and unclenched their jaws, and I could hear someone's change and car keys turn over in their pocket.

These men waited. I waited. It seemed like an eternity, but I estimated that it was about five minutes of complete silence. The air became heavy and thick. We were all tired. I was overwhelmed, and we all wanted this day to end. I thought about these legal professionals and law enforcement officers, all destined to return to their homes tonight. They may even see friends or family members, but I would return to a concrete cell to ponder my fate.

The next few hours were drudgery for me. I signed my name on the interrogation statement and held on to the belief that if I told the truth, things would go more smoothly. Some of the detectives reassured me of that. There was no way for me to grasp the reality or gravity of my situation. At the trial, I knew my own words would eventually be used against me, securing an easy conviction.

I was arraigned the following day. Some of the victim's friends and family members were present. I don't recall ever looking up at the judge or anyone else. My eyes were constantly filled with tears. The only word I spoke was yes when asked if I understood why this legal proceeding was taking place.

Shortly after, the court officials and police detail ushered me out, pushing past the media frenzy. They politely interacted with me as the police placed me in a vehicle. They would put me in a solitary cell for a standard 72-hour period quarantine. That afternoon, a total stranger, a stocky man, approached the tray slot in my cell and offered me tobacco, coffee, and snacks. This was unexpected yet welcomed in an environment where nothing came for free. I had no idea what to expect, but I knew I had no family support and few friends. I would have to face this situation alone—a face-to-face trial followed by a lengthy prison sentence—or so I thought.

The first month or two went by without incident. I spent most of my days waiting on my bunk, thinking about how it would all turn out. I was depressed. Sound sleep was hard to find. When I did sleep, I often had nightmares. My court-appointed attorneys assured me we had ample time to prepare a defense.

That fall, construction ended on a new jail next to the one I was in, and I was transferred there shortly after. There was a new system in place, new guards, and adjustments everywhere.

I had the tendency to be drawn into negative behavior through peer pressure. This began a long period of acting out. I didn't think I had much to lose. Over six months, I had roughly 80 disciplinary reports, which became sort of a joke between the guards and me. In the end, we appeased one another; they wouldn't take away too many privileges, and I would not act out too much.

My court dates began to be more frequent. It seemed like my attorneys and I were always either preparing for a hearing or reviewing recent developments of a new motion or court appearance. Believe it or not, I had some measure of confidence in the justice system and my attorneys. The argument in my case did not hinge on guilt but on intent. The question was regarding the intent of my actions and the state of my mind and emotions when the event occurred. For a while, the idea of a trial seemed promising to me. I was convinced that once my side of the story—the truth—was told, there would be some understanding.

My nightmares became less frequent, but I was still in despair. There was no one I could turn to for advice, comfort, or reassurance. *That would soon change.*

From the time I was adopted and flown from Costa Rica to America, my adoptive family had attended a local church built in the 1800s in a small town in New England. Everyone knew everyone. Two of my family's acquaintances were the organist and choir director and his wife. I remember watching him pump the pedals while he played. My brother and I always paid him a visit at the end of the service, intrigued by the organ, and then we all filed downstairs where refreshments were served.

It had been at least eight years since I had attended a service or had seen this couple. Imagine my initial surprise and heartfelt joy when one winter afternoon I received a letter from this man—Winston. I was amazed, given the fact that my adoptive family had abandoned me long ago. And this man was writing out of concern. He and his wife took it upon themselves to inquire about my well-being. They asked about my lawyer's effectiveness, and I tried to fill them in. I wasn't sure if they knew my adoptive family was not speaking to me, and I didn't want to be a bother. I told them I thought I had a fighting chance.

I was constantly anxious and reactive rather than contemplative. My biggest insecurity was that others would give up on me. The first time I was spotted by social workers in Costa Rica, I was half-naked, playing in the mud on the side of the road. There was no adult to be found for miles. I had been abandoned in more than a physical sense. I made it a practice to keep a distance between myself and others. Even when a person's intentions appeared to be good, I had decided that it was not worth the risk of repeated, painful rejection. Relationships throughout my life had seemed safer on my terms, which explains why I often self-sabotaged.

Soon, the choir director and his wife introduced me to their daughter Karen. Although she was a grown woman, she visited me with her mother and father, at least initially. She made it a point to write to me consistently, and her letters made a substantial difference in my daily existence. These three strangers developed an interesting relationship with me during my time in county jail. At that time, visits were over the phone and through glass, two people at a time. Most often, Winston and his daughter came, and one stood while one sat, sharing the phone. They visited me off and on for months.

My friend's parents also visited me during this time. These few people were who God placed in my life. They were just enough to keep hope alive.

Chapter 8
THE WORST EXPERIENCE, THE BEST RESULT

It was the beginning of my fifth month in county jail—150 days to be exact. Time has a way of moving very slowly when you are held hostage, waiting for an unknown outcome. Although I had been given the advice not to keep track of or count my time in jail, it was an activity I could busy myself with to maintain some semblance of sanity.

I developed a habit of staring through my tray slot for what seemed like hours, but it was probably only minutes. My one hour of freedom was in the afternoon, and for the other 23 hours, I was locked down. I could also go to the day room and have face-to-face conversations with other inmates and then have a cursory five-minute shower. After that, I was hustled back to my cell. I am thoroughly convinced that a person learns to adapt to his or her environment. Whether it's in a desert, a city, a rain forest, or a tightly controlled maximum security correctional facility, I believe a person can adapt.

I spent countless hours counting the array of cracks on the ceiling and the number of concrete blocks (48) my wall was made of. The squeaky wheels of the food cart were a welcome sound. Due to the portion size and lack of substance, I could devour anything served. Sometimes I collected my empty milk cartons, gave them a rinse, and let them dry. By ripping off the top and carefully separating the four sides, I eventually had enough material to make playing cards. It was one more thing to do.

I did have a new variable in my life to consider—the few people who seemed to be taking an unusual interest in me. We exchanged letters, continued visits, and developed new relationships, which were nice surprises for me. Every week, I longed for Thursday night, the visiting time, to roll around. I looked forward to news of the outside world and so much of the life I was missing. My visitors and I enjoyed our time together and our many lighthearted moments.

Karen, the woman I already mentioned, was a quiet, gentle, and loyal individual who was placed in my life for a very special purpose. We would weather together the greatest storm of my life.

Numerous court hearings went by; they were long and arduous for me. There was always a general buzz in the jail when word got out that someone had a hearing. When my turn came, the guards moved me to a holding area in the jail where I waited for the sheriffs who shackled, handcuffed, and chained me. If you knew me now, this is actually humorous, but it wasn't then. I learned to shuffle along and take my time getting in and out of the vehicle to avoid taking a nosedive onto the pavement. The courthouse was only a half mile away, but it seemed much farther. All four of us—the driver, two guards, and I—took the elevator up from the basement entrance to a long corridor where there were attorneys, reporters, and other members of the media congregating in the hallway. This scene made my stomach churn since I did not like cameras and microphones pointed at me. I always remained silent.

We then entered a small, enclosed waiting area. It was there that I saw Karen outside the jail for the first time. She was doing her best to smile and put on a strong, encouraging face. There in a sea of men and women in dark suits, Karen stood out. As we got closer, she stepped out of the crowd and asked the sheriff, so innocently, if she could hug me. Of course, he barked an abrupt "No, ma'am!" and she backed away, crestfallen.

The sheriff ushered me quickly into a small room to meet with my attorney. When it was time to enter the courtroom, there was a stiffness, perhaps heaviness, of power and authority in the air. During the hearing, I glanced over my shoulder, and it was reassuring to see Karen. I was amazed and comforted by her presence four rows behind my counsel. At times, my friend's mother or a woman from my church would come, and sometimes Karen's parents or a friend of hers were there. These people were there to support me, pure and simple. I often asked myself why. What did they have to gain? They didn't owe me anything. In my darkest hour, my adoptive family had abandoned me once again. Ann, my adoptive mother, was on the other side of the aisle waiting to testify against me. But this small group of people gave me the hope that I might not always be alone, no matter the verdict. I might survive this ordeal.

There were many nights I spent tossing and turning, meditating on my fate. My stomach was constantly in knots. The time for the trial was rapidly approaching, and my attorneys gave me no indication of any possible outcome. Jail seemed like a continuation of my life so far—never knowing what might happen next, unable to put my trust in anyone, and nowhere to call home for more than a few months. I responded in the only way I knew how, setting a path of self-destruction. I pushed buttons and became belligerent toward staff. Somewhere along the way, I learned that I didn't have anything to lose, which was all I needed to justify my actions. Outbursts were followed by more outbursts. I even planned to escape and almost succeeded.

Oddly enough, even when I was acting out, some of those people who were supporting me stood by me. Others encouraged me to channel my anger into writing or journaling, which I enjoyed. Karen's mother, Grace, encouraged me to write poetry, a pastime I still enjoy to this day. Some of those pursuits saved me from self-imposed brutal consequences. I also voraciously read any book I could get my hands on, and that is how the love of God started to seep into my consciousness.

The wheels of justice move ever so slowly. My attorneys and I met for hours and hours, reading and rereading mountains of paperwork and some less important evidence. I was always numb and in shock. When my trial began, I could not shake the nervous energy as I heard testimony after testimony. Each day, the courtroom air-conditioning was on full blast, and the cold left me feeling even emptier inside. My small group of friends was still there supporting and encouraging me day by day, no matter how gruesome the details became and how harsh the opposing counsel was.

I never got to speak. My attorneys decided not to put me on the stand, even though I was not fortunate enough to have a jury of my peers or much of the other usual legal rights. I did, however, get to hear my adoptive mother testify against me and other witnesses say things I knew were not true. It really came down to which side had the strongest argument and which parts of my past they would dredge up, but my attorneys cautioned me not to open Pandora's box. If I didn't speak, messing up my attorneys' plan would be hard to do. I never denied my guilt, but I also never had the chance to explain that I did not premeditate this tragic event.

Near the end of the three-day trial, the jury and the victim's family entered the courtroom first, and a small contingent of law students and my few supporters came in next. A large detail of state police then somberly led me in and formed a semicircle around me. The judge gave the jury their instructions (I later learned the instructions were incorrect), and they went into deliberation. My guards whisked me back to county jail.

Two days later, the jury had a verdict, so I returned to the courtroom. I stood at the front of the courtroom, time feeling as if it had suspended. The jury foreperson gave the verdict to the judge, who read it along with the charge. Without any expression, the judge then sentenced me to an automatic life sentence.

I held my breath and stared straight ahead as the harsh words cut through me like a knife. I had just been found guilty of first-degree murder, and under state statutes, that meant a life sentence without parole. I could not even blink. As my mind began to process what I had heard, applause erupted from the prosecution and the victim's family and friends. My adoptive parents joined them. My few but faithful supporters and attorneys were silent. I felt hands steadying my shoulders and grabbing my wrists to snap on the handcuffs. I looked at my expressionless attorneys and then at the floor.

After I was ushered out of the courtroom, I was placed in a vehicle and taken to the state prison where I would remain for my foreseeable future. It was a year and two weeks after that fateful night. For the next week or so, I remained numb. I knew this was a defining moment in my life, and I decided to see this process out, a choice that would ultimately make my prison sentence go a lot smoother. I began to listen and gauge the emotional state of others. There were many situations in which the outcome would depend on my reaction, so I had to learn to step back, assess, and think before I acted. This approach was a new concept for me, but many hours in isolation had turned me into an organized man. I possessed the motivation to get something done, even if my focus wasn't necessarily where it should be.

As my new "family" of supporters began to visit, write letters, and accept my phone calls, I was in a state of shock. What a change! The few material possessions I had grew as generous hearts poured themselves into my life, and I experienced unconditional love, kindness, and support for the first time in my life. There were individuals God placed in my path, even if only briefly, who really helped me. Some were an encouragement to me, and others became a permanent part of the new realm that began to unfold before me.

My first four years in prison were marked by a lot of reading and studying. I was convinced that, given enough time, I could learn and attain wisdom. I also yearned to attain knowledge. I bounced from Buddhism to Taoism, ESP, Chakra system, and any other spiritual practice I could get my hands on. I had been raised in a religious home but had found no form of personal relationship with God. Whatever it was that was out there remained distant and aloof. A soul's only hope was to spend a lifetime searching for wisdom and knowledge of some higher power. I was convinced that then, and only then, could a person ever contemplate the true existence of God.

I wandered on this path for a year or more. It seemed like the harder I tried to search for answers, the more questions I had when I moved on to my next quest. I had serious doubts and searched harder and harder for concrete truths, and thus began my study of Judaism, Mysticism, Islam, and Christianity. I read the Qur'an and immersed myself in Islam for a short time. It required a lot of time and energy with its structure and militant lifestyle, which I had a lot of. I even considered converting.

The choir director and his wife—Karen's parents—were still visiting me. They were born-again Christians who brought the love of God with them whenever they came. I shared my views with them and engaged in discussions with Karen as well. No one judged me or forced me to reconsider my new knowledge, but they continually encouraged me to seek the truth in love.

After studying some radical literature, I decided Islam was not for me. This was my burning question: How does one know if they will enter into Paradise? There is no guarantee that a Muslim will go to heaven. And forgiveness was hard to come by (I saw no mention of grace). My spirit needed something more concrete. I could not leave my soul to chance for all eternity.

I took a break from my spiritual searching and began to express myself through writing. I have always enjoyed writing and reading the writing of others, and Karen had been the single most consistent factor in my life since my trial. She described our growing friendship and appreciation for each other in a poem she penned in May 2007.

The Cracking of the Stone

Two years ago, I made a friend
    Unlikely as he was
He's changed my life forever now
    And is my one true love.

He told a lot of stories then
    With nothing much to say
He slowly let me glimpse inside
    His heart had turned to gray.

I stood by him in many ways
    Like he'd never seen before
I watched him cry, inside and out
    A prisoner of his own war.

I prayed for him and stayed by him
    We wrote and used the phone
Then after Christmas of '05
    A cracking of the stone.

Hugs became longer, hands held tighter
    Through visits three hours long
At the end of February, cold and dark,
    The embers were aglow.

His lips met mine, our worlds collided
    Courses altered all at once.
Since then our lips don't want to part
    Our bodies are as one.

FREE INDEED

I love this man and he loves me
    Soul mates from the start.
We give life and love so freely now
    We can't be torn apart.

Our passion reaches highest heights
    Our growth beyond compare
He's asked me now to be his wife
    Our worlds we want to share.

There's no place else I'd rather be
    Nor man to be beside
I consent so happily
    And long to be your bride.

You can see her insight and incredible clarity of the situation. Even with obstacles and limited resources, we blossomed. Our love grew and grew, and I can confidently say it is still growing today.

I began to look at Karen in a whole new light. She was no longer just a person reaching out trying to break my fall. This woman was a person who was genuinely concerned about me and my well-being. Karen has always wanted the best for me.

Chapter 9
ANGEL TO ME

Our romance continued for a couple more years. We joked about marriage, and one time I even asked Karen to be my wife. She declined, gracefully, stating it wasn't time and we weren't ready yet. Although I really didn't understand what she meant, I wasn't upset because I knew we were best friends. What was the rush? I wasn't going anywhere.

Deep in my heart, though, my fear of abandonment was still at work, and I wondered if she would leave me. I saw it happen all around me—wives and girlfriends gave up on their men and found someone else. I can't say it didn't worry me back then.

My legal situation was not improving. We couldn't catch a break. Lawyers and law clerks alike told me I had valid issues of both a technical and legal nature I could pursue. We hired an attorney, but yet another door slammed shut. Every avenue we took led to a dead end. I was livid. Why did the justice system ignore the facts? Why wasn't justice being pursued? Why was I alienated from the last of my family and friends? Why was I penniless with a tiny window of time closing in on me for appeals? I sank into depression. My attorneys and I put together dozens of letters, emails, and other mailings and sent them to congressmen, the military, foreign embassies, and even experts on PTSD (post-traumatic stress disorder) due to my past experiences. Karen paid for an evaluation by one expert who told us what we already knew but then refused to testify on my behalf. He did provide a report that documented his findings. My candle of hope was quickly melting down, and soon the flame would be extinguished. But I would learn that these self-directed efforts were failing because it was not God's timing, and I had not given my life completely to Him. I became angry at God. I could stay out of trouble, at least by prison standards, but not in God's eyes.

Karen waited patiently and even stood by me in my foolishness, which was a miracle. Looking back now, I cannot stress the importance of God's timing. We may do well to step aside from time to time and ask ourselves if we are being led by our desires or by God's plan (Prov. 3:5–6).

I tried to put on a good front for Karen, but of course she knew me well by then. I would have bouts of anger and frustration, attempting to self-sabotage. I had done it all my life. I even tried to push her away. What I didn't know was that God had put her in my life for a reason. Her love would not quit. The loneliness she endured, the tears she shed, and even the financial distress were all in Jesus's name. I was her assignment. Even she did not know the full extent of the war she was waging. I wrote this poem about her.

ANGEL TO ME

I wonder about our hearts sometimes and whether it's possible to compare them. Let us see:
Looking closely at my own, there is strength and a sense of solidarity
I have volumes of love and large amounts of passion…

Within myself, I feel fear and senseless emotions like sadness, guilt, and remorse. Deep inside, there are heights and triumphs; yet I also see my many faults and mistakes.

I wish I had a stronger heart, a tough and pain-free center where nothing could touch me without my own doing.

I know of one who has a heart like no other. A beautiful, precious heart that has no limits.

I felt this Angel's presence before my blurry vision had cleared. A presence like no other, incomparable!

With a face and eyes so radiant, I could barely get a glance, so beautiful, so precious, without any flaws.

She, this Angel reached out, wings gently folded and brushed up against my cold skin with a comforting warmth.

Sighing, a little less tense: my ears picked up whispers. Whispers of love, promises, and reassurance flowing forth from this Angel.

I wandered up to the chapel a few times. The dad of one of my old friends was a volunteer there, and it was good to see a familiar face. I had a Bible that had been sitting on my shelf collecting dust for six months, and with no idea how close the truth and ultimately my freedom really were, I welcomed a weekend alone in my cell. My cellmate had just been paroled, so I was lying awake feeling sorry for myself. As I lay on my side, I noticed I was humming a familiar tune but barely knew the words. It was "Amazing Grace."

I sat up and felt compelled to pray. With no idea what to pray for or even how to pray (I had prayed only a couple times in my life), I began to cry out to God. Before that moment, I had been in anguish trying to negotiate with God to get out of trouble or get something I thought I really needed. This was different. It was as if I wasn't the one doing the praying. I heard my inner voice, my soul, crying out to God. Grief and sadness overcame me, reminding me of all my guilt and shame. On my knees, weeping, I recalled the words from a recent sermon I had heard: "Whoever calls on the name of the Lord shall be saved" (Rom. 10:13). I could feel my inner being shake as I uttered out loud, barely above a whisper, "Jesus, I need you. Please save me." My heart broke as His peace and love came rushing in. I could feel a tangible sensation in the air all around me and a powerful, gentle presence surrounding me. I had encountered the living God! Tears of joy and gladness flowed out of me as I laughed. It took every ounce of energy in me just to sit up. And so it began for me—I had taken a small yet monumental first step in a new life with Christ.

In January 2010, Karen and I were married. The prison had a dry procedure we had to follow. We could have one witness who was approved by the prison and had a criminal record check. It had to be a 15-minute ceremony, and then the next couple was in and out. I chose a man in my prison unit to be my witness, but because of the inconvenient time at nine a.m. on a Thursday morning, Karen could not bring one of her few friends she had entrusted with this information. So we were few. As I arrived at what I believed to be a few minutes early for the ceremony, I could see only a couple of people in the chapel, and none of them were my wife-to-be. My heart thumped loudly in my chest, full of anticipation. The justice of the peace was present, along with the chapel clerk. I asked my friend to prepare to take a few photos, and then I saw the clerk enter with a woman behind him, a woman who looked familiar. It was my bride! She was wearing a simple yet elegant ivory dress with the customary veil, and I froze in place as she slowly made her way to the altar. That was my cue. I was nervous but could not let her stand up there all alone.

Taking her hand, I could feel her piercing gaze through the veil. My bride looked so beautiful! The ceremony began, and soon we were reading our handwritten vows. I glanced at the justice of the peace, and as he smiled and pronounced us husband and wife, I pulled back the veil to see her radiant smile looking back at me. It seemed as if time stood still. I could hear my lungs exhale as I leaned forward to kiss her. We shared our first, sweet, tender kiss as husband and wife and then stared at each other. Bursting into laughter, I drew my angel to myself. I closed my eyes and took a mental photograph to hold on to forever. What pure joy!

The first 15 months or so after I was saved involved an onslaught of activity that was daunting to say the least. It amazes me now when I look back and see how God strengthened both me and my wife. I had no mentoring or discipleship when I was first saved, and I struggled with a stronghold I had been feeding for years. God has since taught me the importance of follow-up, and I am blessed to share with others the necessity of godly counsel and discipleship. Karen and I were first tried by the death of her mother, Grace, and although her death was not sudden, it was still painful and a major loss for my wife.

For years, Grace had also been a significant figure in my life. She was a gentle, peaceful, meek spirit who loved me for who I really was and accepted me unconditionally. She exemplified faithfulness through writing, visiting, and praying abundantly for me. She read and critiqued my poetry as only a college English professor could but chose her words carefully to encourage and never offend me.

As I have learned to know and love my wife, I see so many of her mother's qualities in her. They share true beauty, inside and out. Grace had a lifetime of wisdom she constantly exhibited by her selfless attitude and the way she carried herself. One of her favorite stories was about when she worked at a radio station in college reading poetry. Her eyes would sparkle with excitement as we discussed a poem I was trying to piece together. We also enjoyed discussing literature, music, and history. She had an unparalleled love for Israel and was fortunate to visit there with a female friend from church. It was the trip of a lifetime. My wife made the same trip with a friend of hers, and not only did she walk where Jesus walked, but she traced her mother's own steps among God's chosen people.

As the years progressed, Grace could no longer visit me because of her health, but she continued to write, apologizing for her handwriting as it gradually slanted upward and became illegible. She had been told the upward slant was the sign of a positive outlook on life. Losing Grace prompted me to write a poem in her memory since she wanted people to celebrate her memory rather than mourn. She was elegant and ever so graceful to the end, and the wonderful blessing of it all is that she made such a powerful and lasting impression on me. I believe that is how a legacy is born. Now, God has gifted me with that legacy in my wife.

A few weeks after Grace's passing, as I wrote a memorial poem, a small sparrow landed on my windowsill in the morning. I noticed the bird between the bars of the window, and it remained for a few minutes. The bird communicated a truth I already held in my heart, that Grace was home with her Lord and Savior, her heavenly Father. And my wife would never be the same. Part of her heart departed this earthly realm.

As time went on, Karen and I leaned on each other. We prayed for healing and asked God to help us persevere. There were many challenging phone calls. She often cried as she mourned the loss of her mother, her best friend, and I felt helpless as I listened.

During that time, God placed a group of godly women in Karen's life who remain with her even today. They became invaluable prayer partners, spiritual mothers, and the foundation of the church my wife now attends. Karen began attending a Friday evening potluck where she was ministered to and learned about spiritual warfare.

A little less than a year later, Karen's sister, Betsy, who had suffered with many health problems, passed away. My wife and her father took Betsy to hospice at a nursing home on a Friday, and she died the following Monday of pulmonary fibrosis. Although Karen and her sister were several years apart and had lived very different lives, Karen was devastated by two losses in one year. Watching my father-in-law endure the loss of his wife of 65 years and the untimely death of his daughter was beyond painful. Some of his grandchildren were masking the pain with substance abuse, and my wife was left to pick up the pieces. I learned that whatever my soul mate experienced, I also experienced. I yearned to be by her side, yet by my own doing I was stuck behind bars miles away from her struggles.

As our foundation was shaken, we continued to look to God, and the same group of godly women continued to love her, disciple her, pray over her, and point her back to God when she needed Him most. There was a tangible sense we were engaged in spiritual warfare, but we had backup in ways we didn't even know existed. My wife was put on a fast track to learning about the army of God, intercession, and spiritual warfare. We began to read and pray ravenously, devouring everything we could to prepare for the road ahead.

The ignorance that had existed in our lives had been bliss, but when reality set in, we were brought to a point of surrender. Our financial situation was turned upside down when we tried to take matters into our own hands and seek the legal route, but we would realize that human courts are not God's courts. We acted before seeking His will, and my wife had to file bankruptcy and was forced to downsize twice in one year and lose possessions she had grown fond of over the years. She experienced discord with her father because of addiction in the family and the grandchildren being enabled, but it was through this season of tremendous financial and material loss that we learned total dependence on God.

We received an overflow of revelation, peace, and prophecy from the Holy Spirit that kept us engaged in expression through art, writing, and ministering to others. God placed a man in my life whom He would use to reveal things to me, but I needed even more (2 Cor. 3:16–18 NASB). I was once a proud, arrogant man who needed to be tested and tried through dreams and visions. My wife helped me understand many of them. I grew from failing tests to passing them by being selfless and open to God's teaching and guidance in my life.

His ways are mysterious and beautiful. I never had a role model in either my biological or adoptive father, but I was being discipled by a man who would become my spiritual father. What a privilege and honor to see God's plan unfold! I continued taking classes in the prison and working so I would not be a financial burden to my wife, and God blessed me with favor at every turn. The Holy Spirit inspired me to paint, and the results were deeply spiritual.

After Karen's mother died, her father continued to visit me with another man from the church who would sometimes come alone. He had been coming to see me quite faithfully since the trial. He had sons my age, and we discussed spiritual things as well as things about life outside of prison.

My wife and I were part of a wonderful group called Aid to Incarcerated Marriages led by two volunteers who had been part of the program for 30 years. They loved the program and the couples. With true insight into the inner workings of the prison along with great spiritual wisdom, they were irreplaceable. Other volunteers tried but never fought for the program, and when other privileges started being stripped away, this program fell on the chopping block. We watched marriages and families crumble and fall apart. Our marriage, founded on Jesus Christ, has not only stood the test of time and hardships but has prevailed and even flourished in every season. It is amazing to witness God's faithfulness in our lives time and time again.

Chapter 10
DELIVERANCE IS A JOURNEY

There is a special bond formed when the Lord draws us into a relationship with other children of the light. It is a connection of great importance in our lives. The road has been a long one to grow in the understanding of belonging to His body, the church.

Freedom also comes with true fellowship in Christ, and all the old insecurity, doubt, and assumptions fall away. As we walk together with God in the light, we are encouraged. Our spirit is renewed, and we have the awesome privilege of helping in the renewal of others.

The Lord has delivered me from an array of issues. I will attempt to describe the details of what has taken place. My family had no contact with me during my trial and conviction, and this absence of support devastated me. I correctly perceived there was bitterness and unforgiveness toward me, but the Lord showed me I had to let go of my ill will and lack of forgiveness toward others. The bitterness and resentment I held on to only caused me more pain. I responded to God's grace, and through this surrender, He gave me a desire to heal, placing a longing within me for something more. Once this change occurred, I felt a release, a deliverance from anguish, restfulness, and peace I had never experienced.

The enemy comes to steal, kill, and destroy, yet Jesus was manifested to destroy the works of the devil (1 John 3:8). I chose to forgive, and in that choice God revealed truth in His power. I have embraced the forgiveness He has shown me, and I have been forgiven much. My letting go and responding to His grace gave me the desire to heal.

For most of my life, I endured frequent moves, changes, and adjustments. I had no sense of stability, and I equated the unknown with fear. I fed on this fear even after I came to Christ since His love had not yet been perfected in me. I was constantly anxious and reacting to situations and circumstances according to my emotional state rather than contemplating wisdom and seeking counsel. My biggest insecurity was to be given up on.

This mentality helps explain the nature of self-sabotage in a person. Life and its circumstances are always on a person's own terms, the walls are in plain sight, and the damage is evident. The Bible tells us that fear is associated with punishment. "There is no fear in love; but perfect love casts out fear" (1 John 4:18).

Thanks to our Lord Jesus, I have a new identity in Him. I no longer need to doubt or question if God has put someone in my path. A child of God belongs to God and has been adopted by the Spirit (Rom. 8:15–16). I now possess a hope greater than anything one could imagine. This is the anchor of my soul.

From the very first memory of abuse in my life, I have come to see the acknowledgment and continued revelation that I am a new creation in Christ. No longer am I a lost boy. There is, however, a childlike wonder I have retained. I love the Creator and greatly admire His creation. It is humbling that He would desire, seek, and pursue a relationship with me. We all seek a relationship such as this, constant and flowing, an uninterrupted fellowship.

I have been so blessed to experience such a deep, powerful, and profound exchange with the Lord. It is becoming commonplace in my life to receive a word or inspiration to write or paint through visions, dreams, and what my wife and I have decided to call "downloads." There is a timing with God unlike anything familiar to this world. When we are granted an opportunity to witness heaven itself open, we arrive at a destination where we belong at that precise moment in time and space. All else begins to fall and fade away. The factors of time and place are irrelevant and inconsequential. The sense of being overshadowed by His presence makes me aware that He has fulfilled my every longing and desire. There is nothing else that satisfies or meets the need to experience Him.

I have a new identity in Christ. A child of God belongs to his Father's household. He has been adopted by the Spirit. "For you did not receive the spirit of bondage again to fear, but you received the Spirit of adoption by whom we cry out, 'Abba, Father'" (Rom. 8:15).

I now have a hope far greater than anything I could have imagined. The terms are simple: by faith I trust in His Son, and as a result, I have an eternal peace and everlasting hope.

Chapter 11
DELIVERANCE IS SO SWEET

What does it mean to be redeemed? Is it a feeling, an understanding one receives, or a physical, spiritual, or intellectual way of life? Are we redeemed, or can we be? I am. I am sure of it—redeemed by the costly, precious, blood of the Lamb of God, Jesus Christ (Eph. 1:7).

So why do I find myself still struggling with sin at times? To understand the definition of redemption, understand that I am redeemed. God brought me to a point in my life where I could honestly acknowledge being delivered. Delivered from what, you ask. Sin, disobedience, and rebellion. Such great darkness covered my heart, and my thoughts were evil, hideous, and disgusting. I lived and thrived on impulses, sensation, and stimulation. I craved a rush—instant gratification, even if it was self-gratification. I never had a life of quality, integrity, or goal orientation, just a mere existence. I dreaded the thought of facing who I had become in the first 24 years of my life. I had run away as a child, trying to avoid so much and never taking responsibility, but in reality, I was avoiding myself.

Looking in the mirror today, I don't even recognize the face staring back at me. I heard the truth: "Faith *comes* by hearing, and hearing by the word of God" (Rom. 10:17). My heart was exposed, and I began to receive the precious, powerful grace and love of God.

The Word tells us that Jesus is the truth. There is truth, and there is untruth; there are lies, deception, manipulation, and delusion. Someone very close to me (my wife), who also knows the truth, began to pray over me with words of power and conviction. I have had a glimpse of what a truly free life looks like, and I am blessed in a very special way. I can worship, pray, and receive impartations from the Holy Spirit through visions and dreams. At times, this spiritual realm is unspeakable, mysterious, and overwhelming, and then I return to my cold, cement cell. Sometimes I go back to walking under my own strength right after a mountaintop experience. What a horrid mess! I seem to be emotionally spent, ashamed, full of guilt, and depressed as I return to the dark side of my fallen nature—my flesh.

Sadly, I slide my mask back on. I am ambitious, a go-getter, a model prisoner. I project all the things I think people want to see in me. I blend the truth and the lie even to my lovely, steadfast wife. It's just too much, too dark, and she would never understand (or would she?). These thoughts are a classic, tried-and-true technique of the devil, the father of all lies. He tries to keep us silent, alone in the dark. I search, yet I do not find; I look in all the wrong places, but only half-heartedly. I was comfortable in my own skin and sin, like a white sow rolling in the mud. I thought I could keep my secrets hidden and out of sight. I bought my own lie. I told myself I could control my sin and that if I was better than before, God would forgive me and accept me. Then it would all be happy ever after.

So Karen and I prayed. She prayed and prayed and prayed. I was angry with God because He wouldn't fix my problems, but my wife sent me books and prayed. She directed me to verses, and I read the Word. I attended discipleship classes and became involved with the prison's church, Kairos (a nationwide prison seminar), and other volunteer opportunities. I began to memorize scripture and became a member of a hospice team. I was even in the position to counsel other brothers. Stop! It's amazing!

My wife and I talk and pray together every day, exchanging parts of the Word we have read, trying to support each other in our Christian walks. While all these things sound wonderful, there was still something brewing below the surface. I could no longer avoid the storm cloud that always loomed on my horizon. Although I could see everything I needed to do, I just could not break through. But then it happened.

In 2014, my wife went to Israel. Upon her return, she told me that among many other blessings, she'd had the opportunity to pray at the Western Wall. Her prayer should not have come as a surprise. She asked the Lord to free me in every sense of the word. During that time, I experienced a period of powerful communion with God through prayer, worship, and meditating on His words of truth and life. For a while, I felt like I was walking on a cloud. I now know this was a glimpse of what our lives will look like in the future—my walk was to be one of complete victory in Jesus. That is the state of my life today.

My wife and I continued to pray over a stronghold in my life: lust. From my earliest memories of childhood sexual abuse and acting out sexually as a teenager to becoming a man addicted to sex, I struggled with this very real sin for years. It seemed there was no escaping it. Everywhere I went and most situations I encountered presented me with temptation. My eyes were constantly wandering, and people who came into my life did not always have pure motives.

Coming to prison just drove the lust into my heart and underground. I thought I could control myself and keep my ungodly desires in check. When I finally surrendered my life to God, I was under the impression that all my burdens and infirmities would be taken from me, 100 percent, overnight. What a fool I was!

Jesus did take all my sins when He died on the cross for me, but it took me a few years to allow God to take control of my life and order my thoughts and steps. It is an interesting concept that when we speak truth and shine the light into a matter in our lives, God will set a plan in motion. Praise God for His sovereignty in my life. I thank Him for His higher thoughts and higher ways.

My wife, the prayer warrior, needed to become aware of the lust in my life since I had been leading a double life and was being torn in two. The devil likes to deceive, trick, lie, and lead us into a pool of guilt and shame, especially with those we love. A secret is only a secret when it is kept in darkness. When truth and light are shed over the sin, something not of ourselves happens.

> *The eye is the lamp of the body. If your eyes are healthy, your whole body will be full of light. But if your eyes are unhealthy, your whole body will be full of darkness.*
>
> —Matt. 6:22–23 NIV

One day, Karen and I were visiting when she cut into the conversation and said, "We need to pray now. We need to come into agreement and pray in one accord." This was the beginning of a paramount shift in my life. My wife spoke to me with directness, her eyes full of an intensity I had never seen before. The weight and authority of her words spelled out for me the need for true repentance and the necessity of being delivered. The Holy Spirit was clearly speaking through her, and it shook me to my core. She put her hand on my shoulder, and with conviction I cried out to God, confessing my sin. As we wept, I felt a noticeable shift in the atmosphere, and I knew deliverance would soon be forthcoming. I had no shame—the truth had set me free. True freedom was on the horizon, and we could smell the aroma of liberty in the air.

Some time went by. I had stepped into ministry for the first time by sharing my testimony at a Bible study with new inmates. Our marriage was flourishing through prayer, regular visits, and an intimacy that can only be found through the Holy Spirit. The truth of the matter was that I was still stumbling now and then, repenting, and feeling forgiven. I had developed a close relationship with one of the visiting pastors who was actively discipling me, as well as an accountability partner to pray with and talk to throughout the day. I committed to be honest with my wife, but I felt like a tremendous burden to her. She sent me solid materials written by Christians on this topic. They were very helpful, and I read them all. This striving is the way the enemy deceived me into feeling like a failure and throwing in the towel. He kept me from the simple solution that God's grace is sufficient, and I had to learn to be accountable to the Holy Spirit who searches all things (1 Cor. 2:10).

God loves us too much to let us wallow in our own filth, so He extended His hand to place me on solid ground. My mind believed I was delivered, but my heart was not completely His. I thought my flesh was the reason or excuse to fall or stumble into sin. Everybody sins, right? Well, I had a serious issue on my hands. I was brought into a season of repentance. I had prayed for this since He had revealed through His Word that it needed to take place.

> *For see what earnestness this godly grief has produced in you, but also what eagerness to clear yourselves, what indignation, what fear, what longing, what zeal, what punishment!*
>
> —2 Cor. 7:11 ESV

God has been so patient with me throughout all these years, and His patience is one of the many reasons I love Him with all my being. My heart is grateful for the mercy and grace He has shown me.

A few weeks after my wife prayed over me and prophesied, revealing important truths about my situation, I believed I was fully delivered. The Lord had once again worked on my behalf. Rivers of living water flowed into my heart, soul, and spirit. As we wrapped up a visit, I began to pray, but this time I had a new prayer language. My wife and I were enveloped in a new form of intimacy. It was like being covered with warm oil so anointed and revealing in the deepest way we had ever experienced. An inexplicable joy filled my heart. I could not control it, and it was so sweet, so refreshing. His presence and His power were flowing through me.

God is so faithful, yet we lack faith. He took all my impurities, my ungodly desires, and washed me as white as snow. My newfound desire is summed up in Him. He set me free!

Shortly after, I had an incredible dream that was spiritual in nature. When it ended, I immediately woke up and recorded the details that were so vivid and amazing. A few days later, I had another dream, and then another. This was becoming normal for me. It was as if a supernatural wave had crashed down around me. Karen and I felt so blessed to have these new spiritual gifts to share with one another. I continued to seek the Lord and grow in Christ. Whenever I prayed in the Spirit, I was refreshed, and my wife would add the depth of a word of knowledge or wisdom that was not typical of her usual prayer life. God was quickening scripture and revealing truths to my wife and me.

Later on, God would show me that this gift of praying in tongues was a direct answer to prayer. I felt completely different, with a new set of eyes. Now, I long and crave for time to pray. This prayer language has also brought my wife and me closer, and we have a new level of intimacy. Within a month, we both received confirmation from the Lord that we must write this book.

I once was lost, but now I'm found. I was blind, but now I see. I was poor, but now I am richer than I could ever imagine. I thought I knew. I thought I had a handle on it all. Complete and total darkness had enveloped me for so long, but now a brilliant flash of light pierced my very soul. The chains fell off—they came off because my Deliverer arrived and led me out. I could not look back; there was nothing there for me anymore. Now, my life began anew.

There is so much to be said about prayer. It has been a direct connection to heaven for my wife and me. We have connected through prayer to our Lord and Savior, and He has awakened our spirits together and individually. There would be no "us" without faith and without prayer, a most crucial component of our lives.

Whenever I hear the term *prayer warrior*, my thoughts immediately turn to my wife. I visualize her crying out to God on my behalf with a myriad of petitions. She has shared with me what it is to travail in prayer, not just for me but for many others, even strangers. What a privilege to be awakened during the night to pray for others as the Spirit leads her!

We have discovered over time that our prayer is not one-sided. God has a lot to say to us through His Spirit, and we have also witnessed incredible answers to prayer. When He calls us into prayer, these divine exchanges are challenging to explain, yet we have both identified that the Spirit has allowed us to express some of these in art, writing, gifts of the Spirit, and dreams.

The previous fall, I was truly and completely delivered from the stronghold of lust. As I stood in a prayer group, I was shown that there were chains at my feet. I asked the Lord what I must do to be free of them once and for all. His answer resounded with tenderness. "All you have to do is step out of them. You are already free; I have set you free, my child." My human, logical mind attempted to connect the dots. How could this be? Faith is such a simple matter. I reasoned that there should be a noticeable difference, an immediate change in how I felt.

As time passed, it became evident that something had changed. I no longer desired to give myself over to the lust of my flesh. This had been a raging battle within me for so long that I had come to accept it as the norm. It was to be the thorn in my flesh. I even bought the lie through the devil's deception that the struggle in my flesh was there for me to learn reliance on God. My heart was experiencing joyous liberation while my mind struggled. The enemy was given a foothold. There is a very real need for us to submit to God and resist the devil.

This very chapter of this book has been held up from progress for months. One may ask, What changed or what powerful insight did I receive from the Lord? I had to take the focus off myself and my condition. When we become fixed on ourselves, we give power to the very areas we are trying to pray against or find deliverance from. But our single focus must be the author and finisher of our faith, Jesus Christ. The reality is that the darkness around us can be defeated. We are victorious in Christ. I now have the privilege and honor to walk in freedom. It is, after all, what we are called to.

> *It was for freedom that Christ set us free; therefore keep standing firm and do not be subject again to a yoke of slavery.*
>
> —Gal. 5:1 NASB

Chapter 12
WHAT NOW, GOD?

With my life fully surrendered, I became my testimony, and my testimony became me. It is only because Jesus died for all my sins and because of the grace of God alone that I can share with you this amazing testimony. We never get the whole picture; we rarely even get perspective, and anything we think we grasp is partial at best. "For we know in part and we prophesy in part" (1 Cor. 13:9). I continued to meditate on this as my wife kept in touch with the Lord.

Lately, I have been comforted by the Lord in all aspects of my life. Because of who He is, I have no reason to doubt. His ways and His timing are perfect. My life prior to knowing Jesus was filled with so much uncertainty. There was an unsettled feeling that clung to me, and the natural response to any situation was to question myself and those around me.

God has called us to a life of obedience. This is neither a burden nor an obligation. Out of our gratefulness for what He has done, we take joy in living for Him. Even more now, I am learning to become a man of integrity and purpose. There is something incredible that has taken place in my life. I give God all the glory, and I continually ask for strength to walk out my faith.

I can do all things through Christ who strengthens me.

—Phil. 4:13

    I am reminded that we are all still a work in progress and that sanctification is a lifelong process. By trusting that He has called us according to His purpose, my wife and I find ourselves in prayer seeking His perfect will for us.

    The Lord continues to place me in a variety of situations to test my response. To what and to whom do I turn? We need to learn to rely on God and place no confidence in ourselves. My flesh has already betrayed me and will do so time and time again, and I cannot trust myself. In the past, I could not handle certain situations. They were too much for me, and as I became overwhelmed, the inevitable fall would occur. Today, through His grace alone, I am blessed to remain firm in my faith and be led by the Holy Spirit (Ps. 112:1–7).

    One of the recent and exciting parts of being made new in Christ is to be used by Him. God has placed me in a body of believers who recognize the work He is doing in me. He has put me in a position in which I am being trained and discipled to fulfill the calling He has on my life, and it is a humbling experience. I have a new desire to not live for myself but for Him. My new life in God is foreign to what I once knew; I praise Him as He shapes and molds me more and more into the image of His Son.

    My wife and I are first best friends, then soul mates, then helpmates, and in some way lovers in the richest spiritual intimacy either of us has ever experienced. We never forget that without the grace of God, we would be nothing. We are becoming one in Christ. It continues to be exciting how God addresses a variety of circumstances we would otherwise be helpless to endure. God has become our healer from the wounds of the past.

    In the words of my wife, we were saved from the trenches of this world for each other. She survived cancer, a couple of car accidents, and other medical issues. We have had many close calls, all to have new lives and purpose, fulfilled in Christ and with each other. We have a deeper love and appreciation for each other with each day that passes. How is this possible? Jesus is in our midst. He is the cord that holds us together. "Two *are* better than one….And a threefold cord is not quickly broken" (Eccles. 4:9, 12).

Five years ago, I thought this must be what it feels like to love and be loved. I realized I had never been loved before. Now I am beginning to grasp what it is like to be given the gift of a godly woman with beauty, gentleness, grace, and poise. She is a child of the living God. I find myself so unworthy.

Our marriage is a beautiful symphony with many instruments, notes, and tempos. It is a masterpiece of God's handiwork with so many colors and designs that it never grows old. We never have enough time to share, pray, or study His Word. We never have enough time to talk, laugh, or just be in each other's presence and enjoy God's creation. We pray that day is coming soon.

My wife and I continue to wait on the Lord. We believe He is constantly at work in our lives. Through sickness and pain, heartache and tribulation, His love remains unchanged and unfailing. It is a part of our lives we have come to know and trust in. We have sought Him and found Him, and we know He has a plan. We have been watching and waiting many years as the Lord has opened and closed doors in our lives. He continues to transform our understanding of all we need to know. We wait for Him in this year 2020, as He may very well unite us if I am physically set free.

The Word teaches us the outcome of those who place their hope in the Lord. Today, I believe God has called me to share this testimony, the truth that there is freedom in Christ. There is healing and deliverance available to all who will place their trust and faith in Him. In addition, the greatest response a former captive or prisoner can have is to bring a message of hope to those in darkness, bondage, and captivity.

FREE INDEED

The spirit of the Lord God *is upon Me,*
Because the Lord *has anointed Me*
To preach good tidings to the poor;
He has sent Me to heal the brokenhearted,
To proclaim liberty to the captives,
And the opening of the prison to those who are *bound.*

—Isa. 61:1

These words touch me as I reflect on my present condition. Today, by His grace, I can boldly say that I am *Free Indeed*!

Therefore if the Son makes you free, you shall be free indeed.

—John 8:36

www.ingramcontent.com/pod-product-compliance
Lightning Source LLC
LaVergne TN
LVHW051527070426
835507LV00023B/3350

9 781735 221717